Accounting 101 Learn The Basic Principles The Right Way

ADIL KHAN

Published by ADIL KHAN, 2023.

Also by ADIL KHAN

Business Strategy Understand What It Takes To Be Successful In Business
Emotional Intelligence Gaining Control Over Emotions
Project Management - Complete Guide For A+ Project Managers
Accounting 101 Learn The Basic Principles The Right Way

Table of Contents

Copyright

Accounting 101 Learn The Basic Principles The Right Way

First Edition: Dec 2023

Book Design by **Adil Khan**

About

In this Book you will learn the basics of accounting. You'll learn all about financial accounting, managerial accounting and income taxes. We'll go over balance sheets, income statements, cash flow statements and much more.

This Book delivers lessons and examples to build accounting skills. It guides students to learn how to read financial statements properly.

By the end of this Book, you'll be able to read the three most common financial statements: the income statement, balance sheet, and statement of cash flows. Then you can apply these skills to a real-world business setting.

Demand for accounting professionals currently exceeds supply. If you're interested in increasing your financial awareness while also gaining a marketable skill, this Book is for you.

Whether you're a sole proprietor looking to manage your business finances or you simply want to gain an understanding of accounting basics for career advancement or for personal use, this Book will give you a solid foundation in accounting.

Introduction

In this presentation we will take a look at what will be included in the not for profit accounting charities colleges and health care Book we're currently in the overview chapter as we scroll through the overview. This could increase as time passes.

We are now in the Book content chapter of the Book as we could see the Book content will be laid out by chapter heading if we select each of the selection headings then it will display what will be included in them. There will not be an even amount of material within each chapter heading but the headings will give us an idea of what will be included. The general layout will include PDA files that can be downloaded and used to go along with the instructional chapters to take notes or use as reference in an online type format and then we're typically going to have downloadable Excel files as well.

After we go through the presentations of the work we will then have presentations and downloadable Excel worksheets so you can apply what you have learned downloading the Excel worksheet and then filling them out in a step by step process along with the instructional chapters below. The Book will start off with an introduction and introduction to government to not for profit accounting comparing and contrasting governmental not for profits and nongovernmental not for profits. Our major goal here is with non-governmental not for profits. However when we do get to the specific areas of schools, universities and health care we will touch on governmental not for profits and non-governmental not for profits for those specific areas. So we'll have the introduction then we'll get into it. Regulations taxation and performance.

This will get in with the kinds of things in terms of what is a not for profit organization and what it means for tax purposes. And as we get into those topics we'll talk about what is required to basically set up a not for profit organization. We'll get into accounting for not for profit organizations as we do so we'll talk about the rules for accounting and then the principles to apply those rules. Our major objective here or what we will be focusing on are those areas where the not for profit accounting differs then from the for profit accounting. So if you don't have any familiarity with the double entry accounting system you might want to go back to some basic accounting Books look at the double entry accounting system itself and then when we think about the not for profit we're really looking at the double entry accounting system when it veers when it changes when it moves away from those areas that we are thinking about for normal not for profits although we will go through entire problems using the double entry accounting system as well. Then we'll go through example problems for accounting for not for profit organizations.

We will look at these in a presentation type format and then we'll also consider them in a worksheet type format. Having an Excel worksheet that can be downloaded and filled out when that's step by step problem along with instructional chapters then we'll get into colleges and universities as we do so the colleges and universities we're focusing in on both the governmental and the nongovernmental as they apply to colleges and universities and to some degree for profit types of colleges as well. We'll talk about the idea of what colleges and universities accounting concepts are and how they differ from other industries.

So there's gonna be similarities between colleges and universities themselves as compared to other types of industries not for profit or for profits. Then we'll consider those areas where the governmental not for profits will be different from the non-governmental not for profits. Then we'll take a look at example problems focusing specifically on the private college meaning non-governmental not for profit colleges specifically. We'll take a look at the example problems in terms of presentation format then we'll have downloadable Excel worksheets and we'll go through the worksheets in a step by step format as well.

Next we'll consider example problems for public universities. In other words the governmental not for profit organizations use a similar format going through it with a presentation type format then having downloadable Excel worksheets and working through it in terms of a step by step process within those Excel worksheets and instructional chapters. Then we will consider health care organizations similar to the layout for colleges in that we'll have both governmental and nongovernmental not for profits with relations to the health care we'll talk about the health care issues in accounting that's going to be different for health care in general as compared to other types of industries whether they be for profit or not for profit. Then we'll take a look at the differences between non-governmental not for profit organizations related to health care and governmental not for profit organizations related to health care. Then we'll get into example problems related to governmental hospitals concentrating on the governmental side.

Going through it with terms of presentation type format and then we'll give the Excel worksheet and we'll work through it in terms of this step by step instructional chapters and filling out those Excel worksheets. Then we'll take a look at example problems for not for profit hospitals. In other words, non-government not for profits and similar formats. We'll go through it and have a presentation type of format then we'll download the Excel worksheet and we'll go through an example problem with the Excel worksheet and step by step presentation step by step instructional chapters.

Governmental Accounting vs Not-For-Profit Accounting

In this presentation we will compare governmental accounting vs. not for profit accounting. First question you might have is aren't they the same thing because oftentimes we see these things grouped together if we see a Book in government or accounting we typically see governmental accounting not for profit accounting grouped together and the answer to that is that it depends when we think about the governmental and not for profit.

We compare that to the grouping of the for profit that's just going to be one format that we can group information together is just like grouping anything else together is the same kind of ideas grouping something like a cap to something like a tiger we might say well they're both in the category of cats but if we wanted to study one or the other or group them into one Book of study we would probably want to separate the two because there's enough distinction between them at this point in time that we would want to focus in on them individually at one point in time they were probably much the same and we could study them together without any type of problem the same is gonna be true with different formats and different specializations within business within accounting at one point in time all of accounting was basically covered by the double entry accounting system.

That's it as time passes then more specialization happens such as governmental accounting breaking off and basically being a subfield that we have to think about separately because there's enough difference to do so and then we have the governmental and not for profit which at this point in time that's a lot of information. So we probably want to break those two out and think of them separately. One to point that out here for a few different reasons.

One Of course is just so that we have them distinct in our mind. So we know what these groupings mean and how we want to approach them and study them so we want to know what we're thinking about when we want to understand a certain concept. So in other words if you're here for something like a not for profit and you run something like a small not for profit type of organization then you might be overwhelmed if you start thinking about and comparing to governmental accounting which is going to use fund accounting.

We may not need fund accounting although some of the not for profit type concepts might apply to other smaller nonprofit types of organizations. If on the other hand we're studying accounting for some formalized studies such as a CPA exam then we typically end up grouping the not for profits and profits together and concentrate a lot of our time on the Governmental Accounting because that's often the one that's going to have the most regulations and oftentimes most complexities therefore including things like fund accounting. If we're a small not for profit organizations then many times we can think about some of the concepts and the objectives of the accounting being similar but oftentimes many of the concepts such as fund accounting may not be applicable to the not for profit organizations and it might be a little bit overwhelming to consider all the rules for governmental accounting when we're thinking about I'm not for profit accounting we'll take a look at that in a bit more detail shortly.

First we want to look at how these things are going to be similar to why we have grouped them together not for profits and governmental accounting. One way we can think about these groupings and subgroups of accounting is to consider governmental accounting compared to for profit accounting. In other words if we think about accounting fields in general and how they have developed the accounting Dublin accounting system would be applied to all types of organizations and then at some point in time as things grow as more regulations happen we break out and consider because of different objectives the Government and not for profits breaking out separately from the for profit. So we have the for profits now being substantially distinct then the not for profit to the point where we consider them two different areas we're going to consider them two different fields of study to some degree obviously there's a lot of overlap and then there's going to be some differences given the changes that have taken place.

What then is the root cause or the key component that defines the changes between a for profit organization and accounting for it and the government and non for profit basically stems from this concept. The for profit organization the owners which we would think of as stockholders if it's a corporation expect a return on investment proportional to resources provided in other words if we're the owner of an organization we're putting our time or money into that organization and we expect to get a return direct return on what we have put into that organization and therefore we are going to be regulating that we're going to be making sure that we measure the performance of the organization to see that we are getting a return that means that the stockholders of the organization are really the primary people that check whether or not that organization is achieving their objectives because they expect to have that market pressure that market return on the investment that they have put into the organization.

Both government and not for profit organizations are financed by providers who do not expect benefits proportional to the resources they provide. So in other words if we think about an organ government type of organization they're going to get resources in terms of tax dollars in order to pay for necessary things. But people in pain in the tax dollars aren't looking for a director's return. They're not expecting a direct return. And the same type of way that you'll have that direct return with a for profit type of organization. Therefore the oversight is a little bit more difficult to see because the people that are putting the money in are not regulating in the same way that you would think that would happen for a for profit organization because you don't have that direct return type of relationship.

The same thing happens with a charitable organization. We put money into a charitable organization to save for medical resources or care in some way or a church or something like that. They take those resources and use it towards some type of goal, however that goal isn't a direct return to the people that are giving the money into the organization and therefore the oversight that the people would typically have in a for profit organization. In other words at a for profit organization we're going to monitor very closely the performance of how management is doing because we expect that direct return when we don't expect that direct return. There's less monitoring when we donate to a charity.

We may not spend as much of our time determining whether or not there is a return. That's not going directly to us but to other people. And therefore the accounting for the organization needs to be in some ways more transparent. It's actually more difficult in some ways because we don't have that market pressure that we would have in the for profit organization. The other way we can group the government and not for profit organizations together and compare and contrast them for it to a for profit organization is through the tax code. We can basically say well a for profit organization is going to be subject to taxation.

The profits are going to be subject to taxation. The government and not for profit organizations are often exempt from taxes. So that's gonna be another way that we can define government and not for profit being grouped together as opposed to for profit being subject to taxes not for profit oftentimes not being subject to taxes. Obviously if we're thinking about something like the government they're not going to tax themselves it would be kind of redundant to tax themselves we tax other organizations.

The tax is the revenue to the government. That's not going to be something that they typically pay if they're going to be the receivers. That's one way we can consider that one where we can define a not for profit organization something like a charity is to simply say that they qualify for tax exemption in some way in some way they're not going to be paying the tax in the same way as a for profit type of organization because they qualify under the tax code for some type of exemption. That's another way that we can define and group and not for profit and governmental together as compared and composed to the for profit organization.

Now let's take a look at some of the regulations as we compare them to our three basic categories that we have. We've got the for profit organizations, we have the not for profit organizations and we have the governmental types of organizations. And this is going to be the type of regulations that we have. We have the FSB which is the Financial Accounting Standards Board. Note that for profits are gonna be subject to FAS the government is subject to fast as well as not for profit. And you can think of this as being similar to weight to the way accounting is basically grown up and how it has evolved. In essence it is being applied to all types of organizations. That's where the basic accounting principles start. Then the regulation happens with FASB as it applies it to standard accounting.

Typically concerned with for profit types of organizations but also flying double entry accounting to governmental and not for profit. And then as things evolved so do the regulations right. So then we have Gatsby Governmental Accounting Standards and this is gonna be where we can think of the evolution happening and we say OK we've realized that there's some areas that the FASB is normal accounting that has different concepts that are necessary and therefore different regulations that are necessary.

Gatsby then is going to be an added type of regulation to fill in those places where the FSB doesn't isn't adequate for governmental accounting. And then we have the FDA as a body which is the Federal Accounting Standards Advisory Board and then it applies to the federal government and its agencies and departments. So you can see here that even if we compare the not for profit to the governmental type of organizations that governmental type of organizations have a lot more regulations that we have to comply with and therefore as these things grow we want to probably break out the not for profit and think of them even separately as the governmental type of organizations.

Given the fact that we're going to have a lot more to deal with as the governmental organizations apply these different types of regulations when one of the major differences between them not for profit organization and governmental organizations is that it's less likely that the not for profit organization will have to apply full fund accounting although they might have other things that they must do to track things differently than a for profit types of organization that governmental accounting is more likely to use full fund accounting which is going to be a system that can be a bit complex.

Does Non-Profit Mean Money Does Not Matter

In this presentation we will take a look at the question of does not for profit mean that money doesn't matter for a not for profit type organization. This can seem like a silly question especially when we're talking about the accounting for a not for profit organization but terms like not for profit can't be taken out of context can be a little bit confusing when we compare and contrast them to for profit types of organizations.

So the answer to the question does it not for profit mean that money doesn't matter to a not for profit organization. I'm going to say no. And then we might ask well why does money matter if the objective of a not for profit organization is theoretically not for profit. And the reason money matters whether it be for profit or not for profit is because that's gonna be our major measuring tool. That's what we're doing within the accounting department. We're trying to measure the performance of how well whatever the objective of the organization is they are doing within it. The dollar is going to be our measuring tool, it's going to be our ruler in order to look at the similarities and the differences.

Let's consider the accounting equation when we think of the accounting equation we think about assets liabilities and equity for a for profit organization we typically see the assets. That's what the company has minus the liabilities that the company owes. That's gonna be loans accounts payable, other types of notes payable and then we have the equity. And this is the value of the organization. And Of course the organization is owned by the owners. And therefore this would be the net value to the owners of the organization so the owners then have an objective to regulate how the assets are used and how the liabilities are leveraged in order to hopefully increase the value or equity of the organization.

The double entry accounting system for a not for profit organization or governmental organization will be much the same and that will still have assets will still have liabilities obligations and the difference between the two. We're gonna call something like net position but in essence we have the same thing as equity. The difference between the two is that the equity represents typically the value to the owner whereas the net position because we don't have a particular owner that can claim value of the net position the net position is the net worth the assets over the liabilities that can be used in the future in order to achieve whatever the objective of the organization is. That could be a charitable type of organization or whatever the services that need to be rendered from the governmental type of organization. Therefore the measuring of these resources are gonna be measured in terms of dollars we're going to use dollars to measure assets, liabilities and the net value of the organization.

The for profit organization is going to be heavily regulated by the market by the owner of the company. If it's a publicly traded company we're talking about stockholders of the organization. And if we're talking about a governmental or not for profit organization we still need to measure this stuff and even be more transparent with the information the money matters more or the measurement matters more. In some ways we want to make it as transparent as possible because we don't have these owners that are going to be as vigilant and take a look at the measuring tools and the objectives being achieved within the organization through that profit objective.

Over here we don't have the profit objective and therefore the people that are donating to the organization aren't going to be the people that are benefiting from the net position or at least not directly. So in other words the people that are donating to a charity or the people paying taxes may get benefits from the charity or from the services that a government organization might provide. But they're not getting the direct benefit that's in proportion to what they're giving in terms of the taxes or the donation as they would expect to have.

With regards to a for profit organization therefore the money in terms of measuring with the money is often more important to be really transparent as possible given the fact that we have less market pressure to meet and to make sure that that money is being managed as well as possible. Another way to consider this is with the income statement type accounts where we have revenue minus expenses giving us a for profit net income. So when we think about a for profit type of organization in terms of performance, how are they doing we think about the income statement we think about how much revenue they are generating, how much expenses they had to take in order to generate that revenue and then the net income is what increases the value of the equity of the organization.

And that would be something that the owner would be very concerned with the stockholders and in a publicly traded company because that's going to increase the value directly relational to the owners in a governmental or not for profit organization. We still have revenue but the revenue is going to be from donors or taxpayers or something like that. We still have expenses but note that for a for profit organization we can basically think of those expenses as something that we needed to consume in order to achieve the goal of new generation when we think about the expenses for a not for profit organization it may not have as good as much of a link that the expenses are going to be related to the generation of revenue as they would be for the goal of the organization to achieve whatever objectives social objective of the organization.

But however the difference between revenue and expenses will still give us the other revenue over the expenses. In essence the same type of net income type of calculation and those resources the revenue over the expenses would be something that we can then increase what would be similar to the equity chapter or the assets minus the liability. What we can then use in order to achieve the goals and objectives of the organization. So it's still going to be necessary for us Of course. Probably even more necessary for us to concentrate more and be more transparent once again in terms of what the revenues are, what the expenses are, and how we're extending this money.

The fact that the expenses are not tied to simply the goal of revenue generation makes it a little bit more difficult for us to determine whether or not those expenses are going to be worthwhile for us to be extending in as opposed to for a for profit organization. The expenses are geared towards the generation of revenue. We have a specific goal and we have owners that are really vigilant in terms of whether or not these expenses are achieving that objective of revenue generation.

Over here we're saying we have expenses that may not be tied directly to the revenue generation. So we have to be more transparent to be able to see where this and where these expenses are going so that we can better make decisions about it. So obviously measuring these items is very important to also note that when we think about these expense items we can also consider who is benefiting from the revenue and the money that's going through these types of organizations. Clearly when we think of a for profit organization we consider the revenue minus the expenditures that go in. In essence to the owner or the owners value then increasing. So we could see directly that the bottom line of the income statement is benefiting the owner.

When we consider the organization in terms of a not for profit or governmental organization we see the bottom line as basically increasing the value to the organization. But it's not being applied directly to a specific type of owner. However we also have within both of these types of organizations included in these expenses things such as wages. So when we consider the money that's being used we have to consider the expenses the value of these expenses and make sure that those are going to be valued well because with it with whatever organization we're thinking about those expenses are gonna be regulated on the for profit side by market pressure to see if they're justified in order to generate revenue.

The expenses with a governmental or not profit organization don't have the same type of market pressure. So determining what these expenses should be can be a little bit more difficult. And Of course included in those expenses are wages. So a substantial amount of people Of course make their money from or earn a living through working for not for profit and governmental organizations. And we need to be able to measure and make sure we're as transparent as possible to decide the proper types of expenses and how they're being expensed.

And so. So these are the types of people that Of course are going to be concerned with the allocation of resources because to the governmental organization it's expenses to the organizations but to these individuals to the workers of the audit organization it is revenue to them. So we want to make sure that Of course that calculation of that revenue the application of the revenue is indeed important.

Regulation, Taxation, and Performance

Within the regulation taxation and performance chapter of the Book will discuss different types of regulations and taxation related to not for profit types of organizations.

As we do so we'll go through the setup process and discuss what types of regulations and taxation what types of tax documents could be involved in the setting up of. I'm not a for profit type organization.

Not for Profit Definition, Organization Forms, & Set Up Process

In this presentation we will take a look at the definition of a not for profit organization organizational forms and part of the set up process related to setting up a not for profit organization not for profit organization definition not for profit organization is an organization with goals involving something other than earning a profit for owners. That's going to be the general definition.

Obviously we can contrast that to a for profit organization or a normal type of business. The default for a normal type of business is the assumption that profit generation is the primary goal so obviously for a not for profit organization something other than profits is going to be the primary goal they usually provide some type of services if it's a not for profit organization success is not measured with profits. So remember success with a not for profit organization can't be measured simply with the profits.

And again part of that is because of the fact that the people that are financing the organization aren't expecting a direct return on the. On the money that they're putting into the organization as they would be if they were in a for profit type of organization. What they want is to put the money into the organization that the not for profit organization has, the not for profit organization uses it efficiently in order to achieve some objective. That is a non-profit type of objective typically an objective that would be for the public good. So it is measured by how the organization contributes to the well-being of the public with the resources it has.

So when you think about putting money for example donating into a not for profit organization you're not thinking okay revenue generation is the main goal of the profit organization or the not for profit organization because you're donating to them what you want when you donate to the not for profit is Of course for them to take that donation and you want to measure how good that the not for profit organization is by how well they take that money how efficiently they spend that money on the need that they're perceived in within the society.

So how are they achieving the goals of providing the needs with the resources that are provided types of not for profit organizations include non governmental and governmental we here are going to be focusing in on the non-governmental types of not for profit organizations which includes either the taxable types of not for profit organizations or the tax exempt types of not for profit organizations. Now if it's a taxable not for profit organization then you could say well it still has the objective that is not the generation of revenue but some other type of objective for the public good perhaps. But it's not qualifying for the tax exempt status.

Most people most of the time when you have a not for profit organization many people actually define. If you talk about a not for profit organization they're going to define it in their mind as a tax exempt type of organization oftentimes. So note that we're not going to spend a lot of time on the taxable, not for profit, type of organization. The thing that's going to be confusing is the thing that's going to be different. The thing that's going to take more time to think about is going to have more types of regulations, more kinds of qualifications in order to qualify for and in order to keep up with the added rules related to , Of course, tax exempt status.

So that's really where we're going to spend most of our time here when we think about the not for profit organizations. It's going to be a non-government type of organization we're considering here and we're typically considering those that are going to be tax exempt. That's going to be kind of one of the points or one of the big issues with relation to not for profit organizations. That's one of the benefits that they have. That's one of the benefits that we have provided them as a society in order to provide the goods and services that they do as a social benefit. So that could include social welfare science colleges, charities , health literacy organizations and other types of surfaces.

When we think about the governmental organizations, remember that oftentimes we grouped these two things together, not for profit organizations including the nongovernmental and the governmental having similar types of characteristics in some ways. As we've discussed in a prior presentation we're gonna be concentrating here once again on the non-governmental but the governmental includes the general purpose state and cities as well as special purposes which would include things like colleges and hospitals. Then Of course the question is how would we create a not for profit type of organization. No. Once we would have an idea.

Typically we would think about what we want to do what we want to do for society would think about and not for profit organization typically that we would be thinking about how can we set up the organization and how can we get tax exempt status. It's probably the types of things that are gonna be running through our mind as we're considering setting up a not for profit type of organization. We have to apply with the state for recognition as a legal entity. So first we've got to get set up as a legal entity that's typically done with the state that's going to be similar to other types of organizations as well if we were trying to set up some type of entity.

Note that if you're setting up some type of business entity, if you're just a sole proprietor you can almost basically just set up and start doing business and you file your tax return using a Schedule C. However if you're some other type of organization such as a corporation, an S corporation or an LLC then you typically start that process out not by going into the federal government but by going into your local state governments and you set up the type of organizations with the state government.

Then you have to go consider that status and that that you need on the IRS side as well so then you have to have an application to the IRS for recognition as a textbook tax exempt entity. So let me think about that one more time you have an idea you want to be a not for profit type of organization. First you need to think about where we want that organization located. What state are we in for the location of that? Then you need to consider the requirements for the state in order to set up a particular type of entity making sure that you set up an entity that can then qualify hopefully for the tax exempt status.

Once you have the entity then you can go to the IRS and you can then apply for the tax exempt status for the IRS in order to get that tax exempt status. So the process is a bit more detailed. It may look something like this. You have an idea. You have an idea for a not for profit type of organization. You want to pick a name that is not misleading and is not used by any other type of organization. So you want to say okay we're going to set up this not for profit.

Got to pick a name for it so we can set up the organization with regards or under that name as you do that you want to make sure that the name is very clear and not misleading at all. You don't want to have anything that looks at all misleading. Of course when you're a not for profit type of organization you want to make things as transparent as possible. That's gonna be one of the objectives of the not for profit type of organization. You can also check with the state to see if the name has been taken already so you can sit. You can go and check and make sure Of course that that name has not already been taken.

There may be some legal offices that can set this up relatively quickly or you can look into it yourself. It's not as complicated a process as you might think to just set up the initial organization; it's actually much more difficult to take down the organization depending on the type of state that you're in. So setting up. But if you talk, take a look at some of these types of businesses that set up organizations a lot. They're usually pretty good at looking up those names checking it they'll say hey give us a top three to five or 10 names and then we'll see if they're available we'll give you some ideas with those as we run through it set up this process then you want to designate an agent and an address.

So Of course we need to have an address for it and that address will help the IRS to know and the state to know where the location of the business will be for you know documentation purposes and tax purposes provide a clear purpose for the entity. This is Of course very important if you are a not for profit organization you have to make sure that you have a clear purpose for that entity. That's going to be a not for profit type purpose. This Of course. And then you could set up with that goal in mind at the state. That's going to be necessary as well as you then file for the tax exempt status with the IRS then you need to appoint a board of directors.

You've got to create the bylaws that provide board responsibilities and operating structures and then we're going to have at least one board meeting a year. So even if you're a small organization you need to go through these steps. And so when you have an A type of organization you've got to set up the board of directors you've got to have the bylaws and you want to have the meetings at least once a year and record the minutes typically for those meetings as evidence that the meetings have taken place.

Management needs to report on financial condition and operations at least once a year as well. Other state and law require straight state and local requirements may include and this will depend Of course on the state and the type of entity application to operate under an assumed name could be called Doing Business As. So if we have basically a name and then we want to have like an assumed name there's gonna be an advertised name. We may have to go through an application process in order to set that up. Compliance reporting this is going to be something that typically will be done on an annual basis.

Application for exemptions for taxes on the state level now because Of course we're gonna have to go to the federal government and ask for exemptions on the federal level so remember there could be two levels of taxes we've got the state taxes we've got the federal taxes when we have an organization. In other words if you were to set up a C Corporation a normal type of corporation and not a pass through type of organization it would typically be considered a separate type of entity a separate type of entity that would typically be paying taxes both state taxes and federal taxes just kind of like an individual does as well.

So in essence what you're doing you're setting up an entity in a similar fashion as you would if it was a for profit type of organization with the state and then you're asking in essence for exemption status. Now the exemption status you have to ask for from the state. So that's what we're going to do here: apply for exemption for the taxes for the state. And then you have to do the same thing and ask for that for the federal taxes as well. So that includes income franchise sales use real real estate taxes and personal property taxes. It could be types of things that the types of taxes that may be exempt depending on the state and the circumstances application to incorporate as a not for profit corporation or a limited liability company.

So once again you want to basically go through the state requirements to set up what is required to set up the organization as a not for profit corporation or a limited liability company. And those are different types of entities that you can basically set up and so you probably want to get some advice as to what the best type of structure for the organization would be. Would it be a corporation not for profit corporation or a limited liability company with special licenses with particular State Departments to operate a health care facility housing corporation residential care facility school or to handle food. These are typical types of not for profit organizations that may need special licensing from the state. Then we have the employer registration. We have things like the payroll tax returns withholding of state taxes and unemployment.

In other words, simply because we're a not for profit type of organization doesn't mean we don't still have to deal with the employee type of situation. If we're going to have employees that are working for the not for profit organization and earning income from it. So we're still going to have to set up the payroll in a similar type of fashion as we would with a for profit type of organization making sure that we were setting up the payroll process and setting up the withholdings for them as well with regards to the state.

We'll have to do a similar type of process with the IRS as well. We also may need a license to solicit charitable contributions, maybe some requirement of the state for a nonprofit organization again depending on the type of organization we have license to have charitable games. If we are to have charitable games then that might be something that we need a licensing process in order to do may have to comply with the Freedom of Information Act. If a large amount of funds are public registration of public lobbyists, lobbying agents and lobbying activities. So if we have those types of activities we have to make sure that those are going to be properly registered. We may need policies on conflict of interest and self dealing with directors.

We may need a notice of any planner plans to merge with another agency. So if there's a planning of a merger process, maybe notification with the state with regards to its license for one day beer, wine or liquor sales. So if there's anything related to alcohol typically that is something that you may need a licensing process for with the state as well license to collect sales and use tax as a vendor. So you need a licensing process to collect the sales and use tax. If that's going to be something applicable again if you're offering something that is applicable to that such as goods then you would have to make sure you're involved with that notice of any plans to dissolve including tax clearance.

So if you're going to close the organization you have to have notification of that as well. Note again this sounds pretty complicated to set up the type of organization but it's not too bad and note that when you close the organization it can actually be a little bit more complicated in some ways to make sure that you have the closing prophecies all taken down in the proper fashion. Here is some information from the IRS Web site.

Of course once you go through the state process then you would need to talk to the IRS and make sure you're set up for that exempt process within the IRS. We'll discuss this a bit more in future presentations. This is just some information that you could find directly at the IRS Web site at this link. So below are steps you need to take before you can apply for tax exempt status. According to the IRS. Again remember what you do is you go to the state first set up the organization then. Now we're thinking about the IRS and the federal income taxes. So determine if your organization is one of the following.

So note number one for the IRS is already assuming we have an organization. And so we've got a set of the organizations that we don't have. We need to plan the organization to set up the organization and then you go to the IRS Web site to think about the tax exempt status. We've been thinking about the state information. Now we're considering the IRS information so the trust corporation association gathers organization documents. We want to gather them together. We'll take a look at that in a bit more detail shortly. Determine your state's registration requirements and obtain an employer I.D. number and E I N number for your new organization. This is a number you're going to set up if you have employees but you're probably going to need to set it up even if you do not have employees.

Because this is gonna be the number that the IRS is going to use to identify the organization. So note that the state and the Fed are gonna be very separate. Many times when people set up organizations they kind of think of the government as all kind of one thing as if the government talks to each other and they talk to each other to some degree but they're quite separate to some degree as well. So you need to go through this process and make sure when you're talking to the state you're talking to the state you're setting up at the state. Then when you're talking to the IRS to the Fed you're talking to the IRS. If there's a problem at the IRS and they say it's at the state level the IRS will not do nothing about it they won't be able to do anything about it.

You'll have to go to the state level and fix that. So you it's going to be the organization, the person who sets up the organization's responsibility to navigate between the state and the Fed in order to set that up properly. Now we'll go into more detail in the organizing documents for the exempt organization. Each application for exemption except for form ten twenty three easy must be accompanied by an exact copy of the organization's organization documents including an incorporation for a corporation.

Articles of Organization for a limited liability company. Articles of Association or constitution for an association or trust agreement or declaration of trust for a trust. If the organization does not have an organization organizing document it will not qualify for exempt status. They're going to need this information obviously to qualify for the exempt status from the IRS. If the organization's name has been legally changed by an amendment to its organizing documents, attach an exact copy of that amendment to the application.

State law generally determines whether an organization is properly created and establishes the requirements for organization organizing documents. So again basically the IRS is saying hey the general rules here with regards to the setting up of the organization documents are typically governed by the state law. Here's a link to the list of states where you can look up that information by state and here's gonna be the state links that you can go to. So if you were to go to the IRS website at this link and then you can go here and go to the applicable state and that might be a good way to kind of start the process if you so choose.

Now we'll discuss in more detail the obtaining and employer identification number for an exempt organization. How do I get an employee identification number and E I N number for my organization? If you can apply for an even number online by fax or by mail , international applications may apply by phone. So there's a lot of ways to get the EIA number. The online application is a fairly simple process. That's a good process to go through. You can see the instructions for form SS for application for employer I.D. number. For further details. Again this is a fairly straightforward process.

The IRS wants to make this a fairly straightforward process because Of course they want to be able to identify the organizations that they will be dealing with. Third parties can receive an e i n on a client's behalf by completing the third party designees chapter and obtaining the client's signature on form. As for this award, it avoids filing form 28 48. Power of attorney or form 88 21 tax information authorization to get an E and for their client. Note: Don't apply for an E I N until your organization is legally formed.

Nearly all organizations are subject to automatic revocation of their tax exempt status if they fail to file a required return or notice for for three consecutive years so three consecutive years that you have a problem or more of a problem when you apply for an E I N we presume you were legally formed and the clock starts running on this three year time period. And here's some more detail on how to create a not for profit organization. IRS type of tax exempt status you can find this at the link below.

Once you have followed the steps outlined in this page you will need to determine what type of tax exempt status you want. So we have charitable religious and educational organizations and you can look into more information here. Social welfare organizations 5 or 1 c 4 organizations as opposed to the 5 or 1 c 3 organizations.

This Of course refers to the IRS code so you can take a look at the actual code. If you would like to add the 5 a 1 c 3 and other non-profit or tax exempt organizations 5 0 1 8 we'll talk about these in a bit more detail in future presentations. But if you want to look into the IRS Web site to read through there you can take a look at the link from here.

Tax Exempt Status & Federal Regulations

In this presentation we will discuss tax exempt status and federal regulations tax exemptions that are possible include things such as sales tax property tax excise tax employment tax and transfer tax. The non-profit organization is going to have similar type of rules that are governing all types of business entities so general laws for businesses not for profits must follow as well include things such as the Fair Labor Standards older workers benefit protection equal employment opportunity.

Disabilities Act the Civil Rights Act drug free workplace laws the immigration laws anti-discrimination laws harassment laws veterans protection and whistleblower protection. We're not going to go into these and a lot of detail because again these are going to be the types of laws that are going to be needed to be followed. Whether we are not for profit type of organization or a normal type of business organization tax exempt status even though an organization is generally granted tax exempt status by a state it still needs to apply to the IRS for tax exempt status unless it is a religious organization such as churches synagogues temples mosques and auxiliaries of religious organizations or any organization with notable gross receipts in a taxable year less than 5000.

The stated purpose of the not for profit organization as well as the services the not for profit will perform determine the Internal Revenue Code. The IRS chapter where it requests exemption status. In other words what the organization's purpose is is going to drive what type of code it might fall under with regards to exemption status for the IRS. You want to consider when you're thinking about setting up the not for profit organization. What type of code you are going to fall in under as you go through this set up process.

The organizational test for tax exempt status is that the Articles of Incorporation must limit the organization's purposes to those described in chapter 5 a one cannot benefit private interests and cannot attempt to influence legislation as a substantial part of its services. So first we'll take a look at the tax exempt status under chapter 5 a one C three so you can actually go to the IRS website you can look up 5 or 1 c 3. If you refer to a type of nonprofit organization. They may be first referred to as 5 or 1 C or 5 or 1 c 3 types of organizations. Those would include charitable organizations, religious organizations, scientific audit organizations, literary organizations and education organizations. Is a very common form of tax exempt type of organization.

This list all fell under the IRS Code chapter 5 a 1 c 3 public charities and private foundations private foundations versus public charities the private foundations include chapter 5 a 1 c 3 organizations unless excluded. They generally have support from a small number of donors and investment income. Most file Form 990 APF and are subject to excise tax. When considering the public charities on the other hand they must meet exclusion and requirements including the public support test and nature of mission and they are not subject to excise taxes lobbying and political activities and lobbying and political activity and not for profit organization can be organized specifically as political parties campaign committees or political action committees.

Most non-profit organizations do not exist for political or lobbying purposes. So in other words once again most non-profit organizations aren't there or don't have an existence for lobbying and political purposes although there is an exception in that they can be set up specifically for these items. The political parties, the campaign committees and the political action committees. So when you think about nonprofit organizations you want to consider in your mind is this a politically set up nonprofit organization.

In one of these three items or some non-political type of nonprofit organization. If it's not a political nonprofit organization they need to be careful about their political activities. So these nonprofit organizations need to be aware of what constitutes allowable and UNallowable lobbying and political activity. So note there should be a distinction there for not a political nonprofit organization. We need to be careful when venturing into a kind of political type of activities because that's not the goal or the objective of the organization.

In chapter 527 political organizations and again this was an IRS code chapter so you could look at this in the Internal Revenue Code chapter 527 political action committees PACs political parties campaign organizations they need to meet organizational tests and they have campaign finance reform requirements of needs to notify the IRS of chapter 527. Elections to when they elect under chapter 527 need to periodically report names and addresses of the donors. So note this is gonna be a nonprofit organization that needs to be very transparent and a political nonprofit organization chapter 527 which needs to be more transparent in some ways. So what if you are not a political entity or political not profit organization.

What's going to be permitted and what's not going to be permitted with regards to political activity. So not permitted activity participating in any political campaign on behalf of or in opposition to any candidate for public office. So the not for profit organization which is not set up as a political entity should not be participating in any political campaign because again that's not the objective of the not for profit type of organization. If it's not set up specifically to do so, it is a limited type of action so these are limited actions that could be political action.

Again not for profit needs to be careful of them but may be able to to participate in such limited action political expenditures direct lobbying grassroots lobbying Form 990 annual reporting requirements Form 990 annual reporting requirements for the not for profit organizations except for religious organizations and governmental NFP is not for profit organizations tax exempt organizations have to file Form 990 annually. So this is going to be the annual reporting form now you might be saying why do I have to file that with the IRS. Given the fact that I don't they're not going to pay any taxes possibly if they're going to be a tax exempt type of organization information form information form still needs to be filed and that's not too different of actually than some other type of information forms that might be filed as well for a pass through entity for example like an S corporation.

We still have to file the corporate return even though the tax is going to be passed through to the individual returns. The IRS still wants to know what's going on even if it's going to be a tax free or tax exempt type of entity form 990 needs to be made publicly available for three years. So it needs to be made publicly available again, transparency being a key component when we're considering not for profit types of organizations. This is something that's going to be part of a requirement to get the benefit of a tax exempt information a tax exempt status and Of course lends some trust then to the not for profit organization Ind. with gross receipts normally fifty thousand or less per year can file Form 990 N.. So if it's fifty thousand or less 990 in Form 990 easy is filed by tax exempt entities with annual gross receipts between fifty thousand two hundred thousand and with less than five hundred thousand total assets unrelated business income UBI not for profit organizations that may be assessed a tax on unrelated business income the tax helped stop unfair competition between not for profit organizations and other small businesses. So you'll note Of course if you set up a not for profit organization many people when you hear not for profit organization you hear oh there's going to be a tax exempt status.

Wouldn't it be nice if you could set up some type of business organization and get a tax exempt status because then Of course you would have a competitive advantage to competitors and you can make more money. You can have possibly high profit margin margins. So you want to make sure the IRS wants to be careful that things that are set up for a not for profit organization. If they have a legitimate objective of a not for profit organization then it should be set up and it shouldn't be in direct competition with other types of businesses that are for profit.

Given the public nature of the service that's generally going to be provided by the not for profit that's going to be the general kind of idea of a not for profit one of the reasons there's a not for profit type of organization is because they might be engaging in things the types of things that the public needs but which there's not as much of a for profit type of incentive the market. In other words, it doesn't typically take care of that need. Therefore you need the incentive ization for the not for profit organization. However if the not for profit organization ventures out away from their primary objective and does some type of activities that looks that's more like a for profit type of activity then in essence they could be in a situation where they're competing with for profit organizations and that's not the goal of setting up the not for profit organization.

So we want to we don't want to have an unfair playing field where people have an incentive in other words to set up a not for profit organization try to do for profit type of activities have a competitive advantage and kind of cheat the system in some ways against other people who have a legitimate for profit organization in that same type so the tax helps to stop unfair competition between not for profits and other small businesses unrelated business income is a gross income from an unrelated trade or business engaged in on a regular basis.

Bases minus directly connected expenses which is in essence the net income of that type of activity that is happening certain net operating losses and qualified charitable contributions activities will be considered unrelated unless they make an important contribution to the accomplishment of the organization's exempt status. So again you might wonder what unrelated business income activities will be considered unrelated unrelated business income which could be subject to taxation unless they make an important contribution to the accomplishments of the organization's exempt purpose. So obviously if they're contributing to the exempt purpose then you would think that it would not be an unrelated business type of activity.

It would be one of the primary activities, those primary activities having to qualify under some code chapter in order to qualify for the exemption status income considered under related business income. UPI include income passed from a feeder organization to a not for profit organization in the form of interest, rents , royalties and annuities. So in other words if we set up some kind of pass through type of system where the income is going from some other type of organization into the not for profit organization that would typically be considered unrelated business income subject to taxation income. That would also be considered unrelated business income includes income from an asset that is mortgaged or debt financed income. So if for example rental of real estate where the not for profit organization holds a mortgage except excessive benefits two officers would include unreasonable compensation.

Sale of assets at bargain prices and lease arrangements. This is going to be an important consideration when you think about setting up a not for profit organization and when you consider donating it to a not for profit organization. Because although when you consider the profits of the organization those profits are not going to. In essence the owners of the organization as they would for a business in other words if we set up a business a corporation we would have the profit of the business which could then be distributed to the owners. So we would make revenue any revenue that is generated at some point in time could be distributed to the owner in the form of dividends in a not for profit organization. That's not generally the case because the goal is for all that profit to then go back into the business in order to serve the good the public interest for which the not for profit was set up in order to do.

However if someone was going to set up a not for profit organization and then the employees of the not for profit organization are still benefiting so they may not be the owners of a not for profit organization but they're making a living from the not for profit organization. So it's quite possible for the compensation of the people within the organization, especially of the top officers of the organization, to have high compensation and you want to make sure that the compensation is reasonable. This is going to be a big topic for not for profit organizations as well because when you consider people that run a not for profit organization and compare what they do to say people that run business type of organizations of a similar size you can you can consider the type of salaries that are given to CEOs which are often considered to be quite high in comparison to the average salaries.

And if you think of the not for profit organization people argue that if you want it to be run well then you should have pretty competitive competition standards for the top owners or the people that are running the type of organization. But again you want to be careful what you want to consider, what is the compensation for the people running the organization when you donate to the organization you set up.

The goal is to streamline the organization and make it efficient which means you do need to pay people well to make it efficient but also to make it so the money is obviously going towards the organization's efficiency so the organization will achieve that goal. So most of the money will be going towards the goals that are being achieved so when you can when you look at an organization you might want to consider how much of the money is going to things like compensation of people like officers and how much of the money is going to the actual goal the objective which is the what the organization was set up to do.

Accounting for Not-for-Profits

Within the accounting for not for profit organizations will discuss accounting rules accounting policies accounting frameworks related to not for profit type organizations.

As we do so we will be comparing and contrasting to for profit types of entities focusing on those areas which will be different in the not for profit as compared to the for profit in the next chapter will actually go through example problems worked through example problems recording transactions related to that not for profit organization.

GAAP for Non governmental NFP

In this presentation we will discuss gap or generally accepted accounting principles for non governmental not for profit organizations in F PS In other words we're talking about not for profit organizations we're talking about those not for profits that are nongovernmental not for profit organizations and the gap or generally accepted accounting principles related to them.

The Financial Accounting Standards Board or the FASB FASB has responsibility for providing guidance on generally accepted accounting principles for non-profit organizations. So when we're considering who is responsible in essence for the guidance related to the accounting principles for non-profit organizations we're looking for the FASB the Financial Accounting Standards Board the FASB the Governmental Accounting Standards Board the Gatsby G.A. as Bea is responsible for governmental nonprofit organizations. So when we think about the nonprofit organizations we're breaking them out from them being nongovernmental governmental we hear considering nongovernmental therefore looking to the FASB rather than the Gatsby.

The FASB as opposed to the G8 as Bea FASB objectives of financial reporting for not for profit organizations. Now as we go through these objectives note these are gonna be the overarching type of objectives for fast deal with relation to not for profit organizations. When you consider the accounting for not for profit organizations you really want to start off with the base point as being similar to a for profit type of organization so when one is they are at for profit type of organizations we have our kind of idea of the for profit organizations the objectives of a for profit organizations we're going to be using the same double entry accounting system we're gonna be wanting to report something like an income statement something like a balance sheet.

However, we want to think about when we need to adjust and how we want to adjust or how we must adjust those kinds of standard principles to adhere to the fact that the not for profit has some differences. And so when you consider the objectives that's how you want to approach it that's what I would recommend for approaching them. You start with the baseline of the for profit type of objectives accrual accounting double entry accounting principles and then think about how those might be modified with not for profit types of organizations.

As we start to post and record transactions related to not for profit organizations these kinds of differences will become more clearer and become a lot more transparent. And this is why I really recommend working through problems because as you work through the problems you start to see when you record transactions. What is the same and what's going to be different and then you can get that foundation principle and then branch out to those things that are going to be different. So making resource allocation decisions assessing services and ability to provide services Assessing management as stewardship and performance and assessing economic resources obligations net resources and changes in them.

So as we go through these keep this in mind as we go through and start to post transactions recording actual activity within a not for profit organizations not for profit organization stakeholders it could include people such as these are going to be people involved people that have some kind of stake in the not for profit organization. Obviously donors to the organization are the people that believe in the organization they're putting money into the not for profit organization because they believe in what the not for profit organization is doing.

Theoretically we then have members of the not for profit organization consumers of the not for profit organization grantees which could be another source of funding of the organization as well. Then we have lenders and other resource providers that could be involved. All these people could be involved or have some kind of stake in the not for profit organization.

Financial Reporting Nongovernmental NFP

In his presentation we will discuss financial reporting for a non-governmental in F peace or not for profit organizations gap or generally accepted accounting principles related to not for profit organizations it includes or contains accrual basis accounting. So we will be using not for profit organizations accrual basis accounting. This should be the default type of accounting that we are familiar with. It's the same accounting type of basis that we would be using for for profit organizations.

Generally you can compare and contrast it to a cash basis type of system. The major two principles being the revenue recognition principle and the matching principle or expense recognition principle. So we won't go into that in a whole lot of detail if you want more information on that. Go to just basic accounting type principles into the accounting Books to get information on the accrual principle. We will be recording transactions however and as we do so we will be doing so with regard to the accrual principles both. So if you're not familiar with the accrual principles you will be picking those up to some degree.

As we start to post those transactions a statement of financial position. This will Of course be similar to a balance sheet. So when we think about the not for profit organization in essence we're gonna have different names for types of statements but they're going to be much the same as for profit type of organizations as well. So we can have the same kind of concept of wanting to know where the organization stays or stands at a specific point of time. How are they looking? As of right now in order to do that we're gonna have a statement of financial position similar to a balance sheet. Then we have these statements of activities.

This is a performance statement. How are they doing over time? Similar to an income statement. When we think about an income statement we need a time frame we need at the beginning. We need an end. We're judging the performance within a specific time frame. The same with the statement of activities as you can have performance within a time frame as opposed to the balance sheet type of statement or the financial position statement which is telling us where the organization stands. How do they look from a fine line from a financial standpoint?

As of this point in time so performance versus where do they stand right now. And then we have the Statement of Cash Flows. So as you'll recall once again we're on an accrual basis system accrual basis system is not a cash based system. Therefore we're not recording transactions just based on the cash flow. And so it's appropriate then to have a statement of cash flow because it will allow us to then transpose or rework that information into a cash flow in that type of situation. So this is going to be very similar to a for profit organization. You could say we have something similar to a balance sheet, something similar to an income statement or profit and loss type statement.

And then we have the statement of cash flows which takes the accrual information putting it into more of a cash type system, a cash flow basis and then comparative statements are encouraged. But the comparative statements are not required. Now we'll discuss the statement of financial position in a bit more detail. It's gonna be the balance sheet type report. As we discussed, it's going to be the balance sheet type report. It's going to report what is happening as of the current point in time or where do we stand as of the current point in time it does not have a time range. It doesn't have a beginning and an end.

We don't need to really even know the beginning time period. Usually we issue the financial statements possibly at month end or year end but note the balance sheet itself as of the month end of December if it's a year in December or the year end December would be the same because it's as of a point in time. So it's going to include the Assets Liabilities and Net assets for the organization. If you compare that Of course to a for profit organization we usually have something like assets liabilities and then equities some type of equity as a sole proprietor we would have the owner's equity if it's a partnership we would have partnership equity if it was a if it was a corporation we would have stockholders equity some type of equity. That's what's different Of course with the not for profit organization because the equity usually represents what is left or what is owed in essence to the owner from the organization and nobody owns the not for profit organization and therefore that chapter assets minus liabilities is one way you can consider it will not be called equity but we'll just simply be called net assets.

So same type of accounting equation you can write it as what is generally written as assets equal Liabilities plus not equity but net assets or what's often seen and not for profit organizations and is also useful and for profit you can rewrite the equation as assets minus liabilities equals not equity but in this case net assets. Again same thing as equity conceptually for the organization in essence its assets minus liabilities is equity for it for profit and it is net assets for the statement of net position. Obviously as we consider this we can see that it's telling us where we stand at this point in time. Well how many assets do we have?

What's our cash, what's our property, plant and equipment and so on. What's our liabilities at this point in time? What do we owe as of Tuesday. Assets minus liability is the net position kind of the net worth of the organization as of a specific point time typically reported at the end of the month or the end of the year. Net assets are required to be reported in two categories. So when we consider the net assets we're gonna have two categories of them. We have a net of assets without donor restrictions and net assets with donor restrictions. Now this will make more sense as we start to record the transactions. This is going to be the part that's going to be a bit more confusing.

You'll recall that the income statement the temporary accounts are going to close in typically for a for profit organization to equity. Here they're going to be closing out to something within the net position type of accounts. Net position being net assets without donor restrictions. Net assets with donor restrictions and Of course we'll talk more about what those restrictions might be shortly. FASB standards require that the statement of financial position provide amounts for total assets total liabilities total net assets and the totals for each of the net asset classifications. Now we'll discuss in a bit more detail these statements of activities: the statement of activities is an operating statement; the statement of activities presents all changes in net assets without donor restrictions.

Net assets with restrictions and total net assets for the reporting period. So it's going to be showing us the activity that is going on but we're going to need a bit more detail when we think about the statement of activities. You'll notice Of course for a for profit organization we don't have to deal with this restriction type of thing. So we haven't. So therefore we are usually in a for profit if you think of just the trial balance having one line out you know revenues minus expenses. And when we report the information with regard to a not for profit type of organization we're then going to have to deal with this issue of restrictions and not restrictions. And that's going to add kind of a level of complication that's not there and for profit organizations that's where we're gonna have to deviate.

So the statement of activities then is very similar to an income statement in that it's showing the performance over time. However as we know the performance for a for profit organization is geared on revenue generation. We're looking at revenue. We're looking at expenses in order to help generate that revenue. We're looking at the bottom line. Net income the higher net income is the better we feel we have done. However Of course with the statement of activities that's not the case because our goal isn't to reach a net income net profit at the bottom line that's as large as we can.

Because what our goal is to take those resources and allocate them efficiently. So when we read the statement of activities we're really looking for something a bit different when we look at the state the income statement for a for profit organization where basically saying what's the bottom line you know how much money did we make. Is it a logical type of question to make what is the revenue minus expenses. When we look at the statement of activities, oftentimes we're basic, we're really looking at how efficiently we spend the revenue. Are we sure we have enough revenue in order to clear our objectives for that time period?

Are we managing the resources that we have properly in order to achieve the objectives of the organization? And part of doing that is to track the restrictions. So this will Of course be more apparent as we go through example problems actually build this from transactions up to a trial balance up to the financial statements. So the statement of activities presents all changes in net assets. So the changes in net assets because that's basically kind of the equity chapter the change in net assets is kind of if it was the change in equity would be this change in equity the major change in equity for for profit is the income statement is net income.

So when they see a change in net assets it's the same as a change in retained earnings or change in the capital account which is

Of course the income statement or in this case the statement of activities. So the net assets without donor restrictions net assets with donor restrictions and total net assets for the reporting period. Now we'll discuss the concept of a reclassification. We're going to read through the concept and then we'll discuss it in more detail.

Net assets released from restrictions generally means the reclassification of support with donor restrictions to support without donor restrictions in the year in which the donor stipulations were met. What does this mean? Note that when we think about a donation there could be restrictions that's put on the donation. So if they're going to be restrictions that's put on the donation then we are somehow restricted as the not for profit organization as to how we're going to spend that money. For example if someone put money into that organization it said you have to spend this on a certain project in the future and therefore if that was then the case then there's gonna be a restriction on the donations that were put in place. We can't just spend it on our general type of activities.

We've been restricted to spend it on a specific type of activity. Now once that activity is done that would mean that the donor stipulation would generally have been met at that point in time and therefore the money the restriction is going to be released from restriction because we've met that restriction. So this will make more sense as we'd record the transactions because what we're going to have to do Of course from a tracking standpoint from an accounting standpoint is track that kind of information or the kind of assets and resources that are going to be in restriction the ones that are not going to be restricted and then be able to report that information in those categories. So let's read through this one more time.

Keeping that in mind, net assets are released from restrictions. So we're going to release it. Released the net assets. Remember that the net assets are assets minus liabilities assets minus liabilities are the net assets similar to the equity chapter which are broken out between two components. Restricted and non restricted. So it's the ones that are restricted in some way. The ones that are not. So net assets released from restrictions the one that we're restricted that we are set now saying are not restricted generally means the reclassification. So we're going to reclassify our support with donor restriction. So there is support with donor restriction. So that means that there was some type of support withdrawn and restriction to support without donor restriction. Well that's the key point.

Now we have the support without the donor restriction. With that reclassification process. And that is the item that's going to be freed up basically for us to spend it. And again this will make more sense as we go through and record the transactions related to it. Donor restrictions in the year in which the donor stipulations were met when we met the stipulations of whatever the restrictions were by the donor the reclassification that may be due to either one satisfaction of program or purpose restrictions to satisfaction of equipment acquisition restriction and three satisfaction of time restrictions either actual donor or implied restrictions.

So no what we have here Of course when we reclassify it then we either satisfied the program or purpose of the restrictions so whatever the restriction was it was met to satisfy a faction of equipment acquisition. So if the restriction was there to acquire equipment then we would have met that if we were then to acquire the equipment satisfaction of time restriction if there was some kind of time restriction that was put on it either actual donor or implied restriction.

Next we have the statement of cash flows the statement of cash flows will be very similar for the not for profit organization as for forthe for profit organization the classifications of the statement of cash flows are the same as they are for a for profit type of organization those that have been operating the investing and the financing chapter. So as you recall a statement of cash flows is going to be a statement that it's going to be focused Of course on the flows. That's an activity statement related to the cash flow activity. We recall that we're going to be using the accrual basis method when we use the accrual basis method we're not recording transactions strictly on a cash flow basis. Therefore it's nice to have the cash flow statement as well in order to report that information on a cash flow statement.

You'll recall that of the three components of the statement of cash flows the operating chapter the investing chapter and the financing chapter the Operating chapter is going to be very similar to what would be an income statement for a for profit type of organization statement of activities for the nonprofit organization where basically can take that from an accrual basis and convert it to more of a cash basis cash flow type of statement. To do that we can use either the direct or indirect method. So this will be similar to a for profit type of organization note that when we consider the direct method and the indirect method we're really looking at the operating activities it doesn't affect the financing activities or the investing activities a reconciliation of the change in total net assets to net cash used for operating activities is optional when the direct method is used. So we have an option in order to add this if the direct method is used.

Note that when we consider the direct method for for profit organizations oftentimes there's still a requirement to have the indirect method or some kind of reconciliation process for that reason the indirect method is often used in a for profit organization for the not for profit the reconciliation of a change in total net assets to net cash used for operating activities is optional optional when the direct method is gonna be used. Now just a quick recap. We're not going to go into a lot of detail on the direct method in the indirect method again if you want to look at that in the statement of cash flows the creation of it.

You could take a look at that in more detail we have presentations just on the Statement of Cash Flows but just a recap of the direct method and indirect method. It is gonna be only on the operating activities as we said the indirect method is going to start with the bottom line. So if we have a standard type of income statement you'll recall that we're saying hey we've already done the income statement on an accrual based bases so to convert it to a cash basis do we really want to go back and redo each of the line items or is it possible for us to start at the bottom line the net income if it was a for profit organization and then back out the things that aren't are cruel basis and not cash bases and end up at cash flows from operating activities. That also provides a nice reconciliation you could see between the net income that's reported on on an accrual basis and what's gonna be reported on.

In essence a cash basis. That's why it's nice to have the indirect method because it has that kind of tying it out. However the indirect method is a little bit less intuitive to think about because if you were thinking about the cash flow from the cash flow statement you would think that you would just redo the whole in essence income statement if it was a for profit organization top to bottom and put it rather than on an accrual basis on a cash basis. And that's what you would do for a direct method. So if you were to explain the direct method to someone I think it's a little bit easier. It's a bit more direct to explain that we just basically you know adjust the line items to be not an accrual basis but on a direct basis method.

But you don't have that kind of reconciliation between net income on an accrual basis and the operating cash flow on a cash flow basis which is nice on the indirect method which is kind of why oftentimes if you'd use the direct method. Very nice. More information to have but you still may want to add in for profit types of organizations that may be required to use some kind of indirect method not the case here. It's an option Statement of Cash Flows at classifications on the less we can have the activity or transaction on the right we're going have a classification in the Statement of Cash Flows. Those include the operating activities, the investing activities and the financing activities. As a general rule, when we're thinking about a for profit organization it's gonna be similar to when we think about a non for profit.

However the names of the accounts will differ because Of course the objectives of the organization differ. So when we have a for profit organization anything related to the income statement you would think would be in the operating type of activities investing activities and that's going to be the biggest component. So the first thing you want to think of is it in operating activities that's going to be the biggest component. If it's related to the income statement you're probably considering that it will be an operating activity. Then you've got the investing activities which include investments like financial investments but also includes things like long term assets.

If you were to purchase something like property plant and equipment that typically would go into investing activity, purchase or sell property plant and equipment and then you have the financing activities which are other forms of financing the type of organization debt financing and things of that nature. So keeping that in mind as we go through this we have the receipt of gifts without donor restrictions. So if we got gifts with no donor restrictions that's kind of like revenue to us if we're a not for profit organization. There's no restrictions, it's going to be in the operating activities. That means that we can spend it on whatever we choose that's within our purpose as the organization in general as a whole.

Receipt of earnings on net assets restricted for long term purposes. So now we've got the net assets that are restricted for long term purposes and we've got the receipt of earnings on them. That's going to be going into the financing type of activities in the Statement of Cash Flows sale of donated financial assets with no restrictions is going to go into the operating activities. So if we got a donation of some type of financial asset then we've got the donation. But in this case it's in the form of financial assets. We sell those financial assets then it's going to be in the operating activities.

Note that's different from the. It's not like the organization was to purchase the financial assets as basically an investment. In this case the financial assets were donated to the organization and the organization then sold them. Next we have the acquisition of a building or equipment using restricted net assets. This is going to be in the investing activities. This is very similar or the same as for a for profit type of organization. If we put money into something like property, plant and equipment it goes into the investing activity. It's a little bit tricky to think about because oftentimes when we think about investing activities we may think about financial investments.

However when we're considering long term investments into something like property, plant and equipment that's an investment into the future and that's why we're going to be putting that into the investing activity non-cash or in kind contributions non-cash investing and financing activities. Obviously there's no cash involved here. So you might be like well it's not gonna go on the Statement of Cash Flows but we are going to have the chapter of non-cash investing and financing activities to take care of those kind of transactions which you can you can kind of think of as as to type of transactions you like if it was that in kind transaction a border type of situation you can kind of think of that as if Cash was involved.

You know one one sale happens for cash and then you split the cash in order to make another purchase. So if that kind of situation is involved we still want to see it in the flow statement so that we have it there therefore we're going to put it into the non-cash investing and financing activities reporting expenses by nature and function expenses must be reported by their functional classifications such as program or supporting. So we need to report that the expenses by their functional classification expenses must also be reported by natural classification like salaries rent interest expense supplies depreciation the types of items that we're more familiar with but the for profit type organization the expense classification is reported either in the statement of activities the notes to the financial statements or as a separate financial statement.

So once again we have the option here the expense classification is reported either in the statement of activities directly in the statement of activities the incomes similar to income statement type statement the notes to the financial statements. So we could say hey here's the classification in the notes to the financial statement and give less detail perhaps in the statement of activity or as a separate financial statement. So we could have less detail in the statement of activities and say hey here's a separate financial statement you can consider the pros and cons of any of these chapters obviously if we put it into the statement of activities like the income statement similar type of income statement accounts and we have these different types of classifications within there the statement of activities gets much more complex to look at.

So it depends on who you're giving the statement, who's reading, who's your primary reader. Do you want to give them more of a bottom line type summary statement and then give the detail some other place or do you want to put it all in one place in terms of the statement of activities. The other option is to is to put it into to the notes to the financial statement or or a separate financial statement that will help to break this added information out financial statements notes notes to the financial statements accounting principles applicable to investor owned organizations must be included in disclosures in the notes the nature and amounts of net assets without donor restrictions and net assets with donor restrictions if not displayed on the face of the financial statements must be disclosed.

So once again this is with regard to that different item with the restrictions the nature and amounts of assets without donor restrictions don't have the donor restrictions that were put in place as the assets were put in place from the donors and net assets with donor restrictions the ones that do have Of course the restrictions that we have to spend or have some type of restriction on whether it be timing or the format in which we spend the money if not displayed on the face of the financial statements they have to be included in the notes so if they're not displayed directly on the face of the financial statement that we need the detail in the notes certain policy statements should also be included in the notes as well.

Contributions Non governmental NFP

In this presentation we will discuss contributions related to nongovernmental NFP not for profit organizations gifts and contributions. Contributions are voluntary, unconditional and non reciprocal. So obviously what we're thinking about a contribution to aid organization if we have a not for profit organization we're considering the contributions which are in essence kind of a form of income to the organization to be a contribution then it's got to be voluntary obviously it's got to be a voluntary thing for the donation or the contribution to take place.

It needs to be unconditional to be a contribution. So it's going to be there's no conditions on it for the contributions and it's non reciprocal non reciprocal means that nothing else has been received in return for the contributions or contribution is made no goods and services are going to be received in return. This is one of the more confusing types of transactions and you could see why it could be confusing because you could consider a situation where what if someone was to donate something what if it wasn't even cash and have a contribution and then receive something in return it would be more like a barter situation.

But remember whether there's cash involved or not. If something was received and something was given usually the assumption then the default assumption is that that's going to be a business type of transaction. It's not going to be a contribution. So the contribution has to be non reciprocal. That's important also because note that some types of charitable organizations may have a contribution kind of component to it but also has something that's non constant non contribution kind of component for example if you were to give something back in essence but the price of it would be way over the value of the thing that you're giving back then you might have to consider a situation where you have you know part of that transaction being a contribution part of it not being a contribution it's gonna be really important to consider the fact of this non reciprocal type of nature.

Anytime we have a situation where we are considering providing something back, what is that going to do to the definition of a contribution with regards to the organization. So a transaction of cash or other assets to the not for profit organization or the settlement of liabilities. So the most common form of contribution Of course will be cash but Of course another type of asset can be given other than cash because of property or some type of investment asset could be given to the organization and they could also settle the liability. That's another form of contribution if the liability was going to be settled for the organization as well.

Contributions can be either unrestricted and they can be restricted with regard to time or they can be restricted with regards to purpose. So if we were to donate to the charity charity we may say hey this is a good charity. I'd like to donate the money whatever you do is good. Your charitable organization is good you're welcome to spend that money in accordance with your mission whatever your mission is within that type of organization. However we might want to get more restrictive we might say we're going to put money into this charitable organization given some restriction some condition that condition may be some time of time constraint condition on the money that's going to be put in or we might put a condition on the purpose we might say that we want this money to be put in we know you do a lot of good work all over the place but there's this specific issue that is concern to me it's something that I want to personally contribute to I know that's one of the things that you do within your nonprofit.

I would like my money to go to that pledge as a pledge to give cash or other assets to an organization. So if we have pledged something to an organization we've basically given a promise that we're going to provide something in the future. This is similar if we compare this to a for profit organization remember the contributions that are given are similar to revenue for for profit organization and a for profit organization we record revenue when the work was done something had to been done to get the revenue which means we would have had to provide goods or services at that point in time is generally when we record the revenue. If we're talking about contributions then typically when we get the contribution we would obviously be recording in contributions at the point in time we get them.

And that would be similar to the revenue in a not for profit type of organization. But when we have pledges, notice a pledge is a promise. So you could think of that situation as OK. There has been a promise that's going to be similar to a situation where the work was done for a for profit organization but we didn't get the money yet. Know accounts receivable situation. So we got the debit of accounts receivable Rick's credit to sales here there's a pledge. So we got a promise kind of. We did the work to get a promise here and you have a similar kind of situation in a sale on account in a for profit type of organization.

We've got a pledge to get what would be similar to income which would be the donation. And that's going to happen sometime in the future and we're going to want to Of course collect on that donation a conditional promise to give is one that depends on the occurrence of a specified future and uncertain event to bind the promises. So if there's some kind of conditional pledge it's going to be conditioned Of course on some type of future event some type of uncertain future event a conditional promise to give is not recorded until the conditions have been substantially met. So if there's going to be a conditional promise until the conditions are substantially met it is not going to be recorded.

Now Of course we're still going to want to track this information. So if the condition is met we can track that information but we're not recording it. Why? Because to record it we would typically have to record it to some type of revenue account. And if there is uncertainty, especially if there's substantial uncertainty as to the condition that might be met in order to get the revenue then we shouldn't be recording the revenue in the time period that the pledge has been made. Given that condition an unconditional promise on the other hand to give depends only on the passage of time or demand by the promises per for performance. So an unconditional promise would be more similar to what we would think of if we had a sale on account of a for profit organization.

In other words if we made a sale on account we invoiced the client the work was done. We expect to be paid. The only thing that's holding things back is time. The time involved there's some time of time period. There's not some type of condition that needs to be met at some future point. So that's going to be similar here. There's no other condition: a pledge was made, the promise was made. It's only some time point in the future, it's only a time situation as to whether the pledge is going to be given in theory, so unconditional promises are reported as support.

In the year the promise is made. Therefore we're going to record this kind of similar to an accrual basis recording similar to a kind of revenue recognition type principle when the promise was made even though we have not yet received the cash similar to an accrual method as opposed to a cash method. They are considered restricted until it is clear that donors' intent related to the contribution has been met. Gifts in kind a gift in kind is a donation of materials or service. So if we were to provide a gift in kind it's a donation to the organization for materials and service rather than cash unconditional gifts in kind reported at fair value.

The entity would include both contribution to revenue and an expense or non-cash asset. Donated material used or consumed in providing services. So they're going to be reported as part of the cost of goods as part of the services. So another thing in other words Of course if we get a gift in kind of some type of donation if we're going to use that within the services then we're going to record the item for revenue and then we're also going to be including the expense related to the use of that item in the service. If we're not using it immediately within the service that we are providing then we're going to put it on the books as a non-cash asset as we put it on the books so if we've got a gift in kind and then we were going to use it.

We've got some types of supplies. If we're making sandwiches or we're making meals and that's part of our charitable process we may then get the groceries or something like that that would be used as a gift in kind. We would record the real revenue related to it which would basically be a credit and then if we were consuming it at this point in time we would have the related expense as we consume it in. With regards to this service that we provide if we're not using it at this point in time then we would recorded as revenue increase in revenue and record the assets on the books that non-cash asset that was received contributed services FASB requires recognition of contributed services at their fair value if the services received create or enhance non-financial assets or require specialized skills are provided by individuals possessing those skills and typically would need to be purchased if not provided by donation.

So in other words when you think about the idea of services that are being contributed typically they're not going to be included as revenue because much of the time that the services are being provided they're not specialized skills that are being provided and they're not there to create or enhance non-financial assets they're going to be non-professional skills within the service of the organization for example if we were to put on something like a meals or something like that and the services are provided to help clean up the location and set up the location. That's not going to be a type of specialized skill and it's not going to create enhanced non-financial assets. So it would not then be included as revenue towards the organization or some type of income or similar to revenue of the type of organization.

However if their contribution it wouldn't be included as a contribution in other words. However if we're talking about something like legal services or something like that where you have a specialized skill a specialized skill that is being donated which you would normally have to pay for if you didn't have that donation of that specialized skill then that is something that could be then a contribution so non specialized a general rule most of the donations most of the skills that are being provided will not be included as a contribution as similar to basically income in the not for profit if it is something that's going to be specialized.

Think of the trades such as a legal trade, possibly accounting information. Those are things that could then be included in the non profit as a contribution donation of land building and equipment. They're going to be recognized at the fair value at the time of donation. So you'll think about the land and the building or something like that equipment that's going to be donated to the organization. How are you going to put that on the books? We're going to recognize it at the fair value at the point in time of the donation. They can be donor restricted or unrestricted so the donor could put restrictions on this type of assets that they donate to the organization buildings and equipment classify it with donor restrictions so if they're classified with donor restrictions then the donor restrictions are assumed to have expired when the asset is placed in service.

So if we put the asset into service then we would assume the restrictions to have expired unless donor restrictions limit the use of the asset for a specific period of time or for a specific purpose. So notice Of course when you put land or building or equipment if you donate that to the not for profit organization it might be the case that the not for profit organization takes that and then uses it within the organization or it might be that they take that and want to sell it.

With regards to the organization as some kind of donation that was just not a cash donation and then possibly sell it and get cash for it. So then that consideration is do we put that equipment into service within the organization or do we not put it into service. Special Events receipts from the event revenue from special events are reported at gross rather than net gross unless the event is peripheral or incidental to the not for profit organization direct expenses direct expenses related to providing the benefit and they're reported separately. Then we have the fundraising expenses related to promoting and conducting the special event.

Accounting for Expenses Nongovernmental NFP

In this presentation we will discuss accounting for expenses related to a nongovernmental not for profit organization a nongovernmental in FP.. The expenses will be accounted for using an accrual method. So we're gonna be using the accrual method when we think of the accrual method that's related to the expense side of things.

We're thinking about the matching principle or otherwise known as the expense recognition principle. The accrual method as we know can be contrasted with the cash method with the cash method we would be recognized the expenses when the cash goes out of the organization under the accrual method the expense in essence happens when the item that we are using has been incurred in order to help us with the function of the project that we are doing in order to help the organization that not for profit to achieve the goal. So once we have actually received the goods or service that's typically when it would be recorded under the matching or expense recognition accrual principle.

Expenses will be recorded as decreases in net assets without donor restrictions. So you'll recall when we had the revenue when we're thinking about the revenue there may be restrictions on the revenue when it goes into a not for profit organization. For example if a donor donates money to the not for profit organization and says I want it restricted in some way then we're going to put a restriction on that. However, on the expense side of things we don't think about those restricted items. Everything that's going to be recorded on the expense side of things is going to be recorded without restrictions so we don't have to worry about basically labeling the accounts as either with or without restrictions on the expense side. They will be without restrictions on the revenue side. They may be restricted or not.

And then we're going to have to unrestricted them whenever the qualifications have been granted or done in order to release them from restrictions. Obviously we're talking about net assets here because the expenses will then roll into what would be similar to the equity chapter in this case would be the net assets chapter. The net assets are going to be broken out as well between with restrictions without restrictions. When we do the closing process the expenses will always be closed out too without restrictions.

We'll show example problems related to this and this will make a lot more sense and we'll go through the whole process of recording the expenses and then that closing process of closing these out to what would be similar to the equity chapter. The net assets chapter as we do you'll see the added kind of complication of closing out items that happen with restrictions. Those that do not have expenses will always not have the restrictions and then it's going to be classified by the functional classification. So note when we think about the financial statements we need to classify it by function not necessarily by nature on the face of the financial statement. So when we think about By nature we're thinking about the actual expense categories.

Typically with things like the utilities expense things like the telephone expense and so on and so forth. When we think about a class defined by function then we're classified by what the expense is used for. This could often be very useful for a not for profit organization because we're going to be giving the financial statements to the board of directors often people and a not for profit organization that might not be really familiar with reading financial statements. If we classify by function then it's usually a lot easier or more condensed.

Financial statement and we can start negotiation or talking from that point forward in terms of planning for the not for profit organization and then get into more detail with the expenses then being broken out by function and nature naming the type of expenses as well. If and when necessary. So the functional expenses when we classify these expenses then by function rather than by nature. So instead of just listing out what the expense was used for telephone expense utilities expense and so forth how would we classify by then function program classifications are from the provision of goods or services that help achieve the major purpose or mission so we can classify by program then and programs would typically include things like research information advocacy and public awareness.

These are the types of programs that are basically the objectives of the organization. We can group the expenses into these types of objective type categories then we have these support activities that assist the not for profit organization in carrying out its mission. So we have the actual programs what it's trying to do which are basically aligned to its mission and then the supporting activities that are gonna be helpful to it which are also types of functions that we can break out into that would include things like the fundraising that's a supporting type of item and the management and general so the management and general expenses is Of course another type of expense a type of grouping a type of function that's not the actual goal but it's something that's going to be a supporting goal to get to the actual goals of the not for profit organization.

Joint Costs of Fund-Raising Nongovernmental NFP

In this presentation we will discuss joint costs of fundraising related to a nongovernmental not for profit a nongovernmental in f the joint costs of fundraising. Not for profits can conduct activities that have both a program or administrative activity and fundraising joint costs of these activities that need to be allocated. So in other words you'll recall that we're recording the expenses primarily by function, by activity , by what they're basically used for rather than by nature.

If we report by nature then we would just simply report utilities or the telephone expense and so on and so forth. If war reporting by function, if we have to report by function then there's gonna be a question asked to these types of activities that may have two things involved. If it has to act two things that are combined together in some way such as program or administrative type of activities being combined with fund raising activities the question Of course then is how do we report these. Is there some general rule that we should report them in one's specific function? Or can we report them and multiple functions.

Considering it's the same activity and we have to if we do decide to report them in multiple functions then we have the problem of how we are going to allocate this information to multiple types of functions. So here's the fact that the guidelines for allocating joint costs: the total cost of activities that include a fundraising appeal should be reported as fund raising costs unless a bona fide program or management and general function has been conducted in conjunction with the appeal for funds. So in essence the default would be fundraising if you got something like fundraising and something else you know the default then would be fund raising unless there's going to be a significant component of it that's gonna go into the general function or some or some program. So let's read that one more time.

The total cost of activities that includes a fundraising appeal should be reported as fund raising costs unless a bona fide program or management and general function has been conducted in conjunction with appeal for funds. So that's going to be the default. Next the joint costs of a bona fide program or management and general function should be allocated between the bona fide function and fund raising. Using an equitable allocation base so then it's going to say hey if you have to allocate it between the two items between fundraising and program or fundraising and management and general then you have to use some type of allocation base because obviously if it's the same kind of event that we had expenses we're going to have to use some kind of method to allocate it between the two.

Oftentimes we're going to use some type of allocation based to come up with percentages that we can then use the percentages Of course to allocate between the applicable programs and or fundraising and or general and administrative criteria of purpose audience and content must be met in order to conclude that a bona fide program or management and general function has been conducted in conjunction with the appeal for funds. In other words if we have basically an appeal for funds that's kind of the default setting in order for us to prove that there's some other item that we're going to be allocating it to.

Whether that be a program or management and general this criteria must meet criteria of purpose audience and content. So what does that mean? Criteria of purpose audit and audience and content. We'll take a look in more depth now. Here are the criteria. First purpose, the criteria of purpose. One of the criteria that would need to be met in order for us to say that we don't just have fundraising but our allocating also to program and or general and administrative purpose. Then the joint activity helps accomplish a program purpose or a management activity. So whatever we're looking at it has to have something that joint activity has to have something that will help accomplish the program purpose.

Basically that's going to be one of the objectives of the not for profit organization or a management activity in terms of audience. The audience was selected primarily for a program or management purpose rather than ability to make a donation. So when we think about the audience, was the audience put together simply so that we can basically have fundraising to get a donation or was the audience put together primarily for a program or management purpose program purpose or management purpose.

Why is the audience there then we have content? The joint activity motivates the audience to action in furtherance of the mission or meets a management responsibility. So what's the content that's going to be involved. Is it motivating us towards the mission of the organization? Basically kind of more of a program type function or towards some kind of management responsibility that is necessary or is simply the content is generally for fundraising.

Restricted Assets & Investments Nongovernmental NFP

In this presentation we will discuss restricted assets and investments related to a nongovernmental not for profit organization a nongovernmental and FTE restricted assets restricted assets or assets that are not available for current operating purposes. So they're not available for current operating purposes. They are therefore restricted donors limited their use to a long term purpose like capital asset acquisition. In other words where did the restriction come from when they were donated to the not for profit organization the dome.

The donors had limited their use for some type of purpose so the limitation came from the donor as the donor was to give the assets to the organization and put some type of restriction on its restricted assets should be classified separately from current assets. On the face of the statement of financial position. So when we're considering the statement of financial position similar to the balance sheet type of activity we're looking at the assets chapter and we have the current assets.

We're going to have the restricted assets that will have a separate categorization to give the implication or to show the restriction of those assets. Next we have investments. Now when we consider investments there's a couple things that are common to the question of investments: how are we going to deal with investments. The investments are going to be a type of assets on the books so we have assets related to investments. The questions come into play as to how we record the investment that we receive.

Typically if we purchase it then obviously we recorded at the purchase price. However if it's a donated asset such as donated securities that were given to us how do we value that because the person who purchased it at some point in the past now is giving it to us do we put it on the books at the fair value or some other value. Also there's always a question as to should we record the change in the value of investment. If we have securities that are actually traded on the Stock Exchange they could go up and down and we can know with fairly good certainty what the current value of that is as opposed to something like equipment where we don't know what the value or a building because they're unique in nature and we only know what the value is.

Once we sell it with with investments they're more liquid in nature and we have similar investments that are trading and we have a pretty good idea of the valuation for investments so the question always is should we adjust the value of the investments to the market value the current value at the reporting date or should we be reporting it at basically cost as a similar way that we would do for like property plant and equipment. So if there was a purchase of investment we're going to the acquisition price for the debt securities or fair value for equity securities are typically going to be used and that's going to be fairly straightforward but if we have a purchase for a not for profit organization of investments if we took some of our cash and then purchased it typically then you purchased it on the market and we would be recording that investment at in essence the price that we purchased it for.

Typically if we have the donated investment however that's going to be the situation that's going to be a bit different and a not for profit organization typically than a for profit organization where we will report at their fair value on the date of donation. Again note the scenario that can happen here if we have some donor that gave investments like stocks let's say to the organization as opposed to cash. The question is how do we record that. Because when they bought the stocks their cost basis in other words happened way back when they purchased it.

Now they're donating it to us. Do we take the cost that they paid for it or do we take the current price at the time of donation. And the answer here is we're going to take the fair value at the date of the donation if we have the reporting periods such as the fiscal year end. So the fiscal year ends when we report the financial statements. How should we report the investments? Should we report the investments at the cost if we purchased it or the fair fair value at the point in time that it was donated to us or should we adjust it to the fair market value at the point of time of the date of the financial statements that we're putting together typically.

And the answer here is we're going to be putting it at the fair value at the major date at the measurement date. So when we make the financial statements in other words we will typically be adjusting many much of the investments if it's a stock it's a publicly traded stock we're going to say hey we know what the fair value is we're gonna make an adjustment to the market value to the fair value at the point in time in essence that we are creating the financial statements. Well then the question is will what do we do if like if you think about that logistically how would we do that from a bookkeeping standpoint let's say that the investment went up in value we knew it went up in value because what we looked at the Stock Exchange and we know that the same stock is selling at a higher price therefore we can safely assume that our stock is valued at that price at the date and point in time that the sales are made at that time. So we're going to the value of the investment.

Well what do we do with the other side? We didn't sell it right. We didn't sell it. And typically we don't record income until we sell something. So we're going to have to know how to record the other side. Either we put it into an equity chapter or we put it into income in the current time period. And the answer here is we're going to have a realized and unrealized gain or loss. What are we going to do with the realized or unrealized reported on the current period's statement of activity. Now realized gains simply means that we sold it. If we sold it we realized the gain. And there's not much question there if we sold the stock.

We realized the gain we're going to record the sale of the stock and we're going to recognize the gain or loss on the sale so we're probably going to debit cash we're going to credit the stocks that were sold and the gain or loss on the sale will then be recorded on this. The statement of activities which is like the income statement. Now if it's unrealized then that's where usually the question comes in. What if it just went up in value we didn't sell it it just went up in value and we're going to increase reported at the increased value.

Well we're still going to report that unrealized gain which means we haven't sold it but it went up in value on the statement of activity affects appropriate net asset account net asset without donor restrictions or net assets with donor restrictions. So when we think about the net asset accounts remember that the income that we're going to report the unrealized gain or the realized gain is going to then be closed out in the closing process to what would be similar to the equity chapter which we're gonna call net assets the net assets are going to either have restrictions on them or not to be restricted.

Now when we think about the investment income it may have restrictions or it may not. It's really due to whether the donor had put restrictions on it or not. So in other words the donor could have said hey here's some stocks here's some investment here's some stocks I have no restrictions on it you can do with it whatever you would like. There is a restriction to some degree in the function or the form of the asset that we get. For example if we got a house or something like that or a building we're restricted to use it kind of like as a building we could sell it and whatnot but we're somewhat restricted but that's not what we're talking about with restrictions here.

Doesn't matter what the thing was given the assets that were given. The restriction would be from the donor to say I want you to use this in some specific way. So if they were to say I want you to use this investment and the proceeds from it in some specific way then there would be some type of restriction on it if there was a restriction on it and the income was restricted. Then when we closed it out it would be going out in closed out to the restricted. Similar to the equity account restricted net assets type of account footnotes. We also need detailed footnotes related to the investments.

Collections Nongovernmental NFP

In this presentation we will discuss collections as they relate to non-governmental not for profit organizations non-governmental in F peace. When you hear the term collections you might think of the term collectibles collections collectibles collections are works of art historical treasures or similar assets that are held for public exhibition education or research in furtherance of public service rather than financial gain.

So these are collectible type of items collections type of items not held simply for financial gain but held for public exhibition education or research in furtherance of public service. Protected, kept unencumbered, cared for and preserved subject to an organizational policy that requires the proceeds of items that are sold to be used to acquire other items for collection. So in other words if we sell basically the collections types of items the revenue that would be used at that sales point would be used for more collectibles to be purchased. Collections capitalized collections are recognized as assets in the period they are acquired. So if we are to capitalize the collection they're going to be represented as assets in the period required if we purchase them.

Obviously they will be represented as an asset at the point in time of purchase for possibly the cost of it if they're donated. Then Of course that would be the time that we would be receiving them as well. At the point of the donation of the collections, capitalized art historical treasures do not need to be depreciated if their economic benefit is used up so slowly that their estimated useful life or lives are extraordinarily long. So if we have these collectibles on the book you might say hey this is a work of art. It's not going to depreciate, possibly it will depreciate in terms of its physical depreciation over some period of time but possibly that might be much longer than a lifetime and therefore maybe it's something that we shouldn't be depreciating.

But keep it on the books considering the fact that it's going to deteriorate so slowly that the value of it should be retained for a very long period of time. Therefore we have something on the books that's going to be basically an asset. Usually we allocate that costs with regards for example to property plant and equipment. We may have an exception to that with regards to collections if it's going to take a long time for them to basically go down in value.

How would we know that? Well this happens if the assets individually have cultural aesthetic or historic value that is worth preserving perpetually. And the holder has the technological and financial ability to protect and preserve essentially undiminished. Thus the service potential of the asset is doing that.

Managerial (Cost) Accounting For Beginners

I believe that you should not fall asleep when learning something new. You need to be encouraged and excited instead. In order to be excited about learning, you need to understand easily. If you struggle to understand, Of course you will fall asleep. I have implemented a new way of teaching. Animated videos which are easy to understand. Problem solving videos that teach you how to apply what you have learned. Learning has never been so exciting.

In this Book you will find great tools used in business that will aid the decision-making process. You will be able to identify and use important accounting information, identify and analyze various alternatives (projects, investments), and choose the best.

The second type is a problem solving shared screen that will help you with the calculations and analysis, as well as your thinking process.

Depending on your commitment, this Book can take you somewhere from a week to a few weeks to complete. The curriculum is designed as such, so that you will retain the information you will receive.

Whether you are a business owner, manager, or a student, you will need this Book. This Book will provide you with great tools that will make your decisions much more informative and calculated.

Managerial Accounting Introduction

In this chapter, we will introduce the topic of managerial accounting. When considering managerial accounting, we can't compare it to the other major form of accounting, which is financial accounting. There will be overlap between managerial accounting and financial accounting, but the major difference when we consider managerial accounting is that our main focus is for management.

Our main focus is for management to use management's goal to make decision making for the company. So managerial accounting is geared towards decision making processes, making reports for management. If we contrast that to financial accounting, financial accounting is the creation of the financial statements. Ultimately, we're entering data. We're going to create the financial statements, the balance sheet, the income statement, the statement of equity, and we could use that by management.

However, the primary goal in the way it is constructed is actually for external users. So when we make the financial statements, when we think about financial accounting, everything that we put together is really geared towards the eyes and the objectives and the goals of external users. People like investors, people like creditors. They're not designed necessarily or ultimately solely for the primary purpose being the management. Usually when we think about this, we think, Hey, wait a second, the financial statements are basically all of the financial data. So wouldn't the manager wouldn't management need to be using the same income statement, balance sheet statement of equity when making decisions as would the external users? And the answer is yes.

The management will be using that information. The financial data that we're putting together will be used for managerial accounting as well. But the managerial accounting isn't restricted in the same way as we are with the financial statement reports, because the financial statement reports are really geared to. And there's going to be restrictions on rate regulatory restrictions so that the financial statements are proper and for the best use of the goal for external users. So although they're going to be the same financial data for the managerial accounting, we can do other things with it outside of just the norm of the financial statements.

We can customize them. In other words, make custom reports for management, for decision making processes. So everything that's going to flow forward in terms of what's the difference between managerial accounting and financial accounting will gear back to this answer. It seems fundamental, it seems basic, but everything stems from this, and that is that managerial accounting is for management, it's for internal users as opposed to external users.

It's for the decision making processes for that management to make decisions about future decisions as opposed to external users to make sure that they have the information they know they need typically for investment decisions or credit type decisions. So given that managerial accounting is for management, let's think of some of the differences. And it's always useful to think about the differences in contrasting the financial accounting versus managerial accounting. So who are the users for financial accounting and managerial accounting?

The users are going to be external for the financial accounting and managerial accounting are going to be internal. And again, that's the major focus, the financial accounting, although we use the same information, the information is designed and put together in such a way and regulated to be put in together in such a way so that external users can trust it, be able to know exactly what's going to be expected from it, and be able to uses those external users being investors, creditors and the managerial accounting. We're talking about internal users. So we don't have that same problem of the internal users trying to, you know, print reports that might be deceptive to themselves or anything like that.

And therefore, management can print their internal reports in more of a free way however they want it to create the reports or put the numbers in order to make the best decisions. So most of the differences between these two types of accounting will fall into alignment with this major difference here. Who are we focused on, internal users or external users? Then we have the reason for the accounting. The external decision making in terms of financial accounting is what we're putting this together for. So we're looking for external users, investors, and creditors. They want to make investment decisions. Should they put their money into the business? Should they invest in the stock? Should a bank loan money to the organization?

Are those things they need in order to make those decisions? They need some financial statements that they can rely on, numbers they can rely on, and those numbers need to be based on what they want to know. Big picture. Typically the full company. How is the company doing as a whole? Managerial accounting is going to be focused on managerial planning type decisions. So that means that the whole purpose is to really take that information and put it into a plan for the future.

Now note that there is overlap, Of course, because if I'm thinking about investing in a company, I might do my own kind of projections and try to think about what they are going to do in the future? Do they have a good plan? Is it going to be a good plan? However, really, the investors are trying to see how they're where a company stands at this point in time and might not be getting so much into the nitty gritty as manager or accounting may do to take these numbers and use them to make more detailed projections, especially about a piecemeal piece by piece, unit by unit, area by area, department by department of the company. And then we've got flexibility.

Financial accounting is going to be limited by regulations and generally accepted accounting principles in the U.S. Typically, there's going to be limitations. And the reason for that is because these external users need to know what they're getting. They need some form of standardization so that they can compare this company's financials to other companies. Financials, and therefore, financial accounting is going to be much more standardized. It's got to be in order to build trust with the public. If we're trying to get investments from the public, then we have to be in alignment with standards that the public can expect so that they can read what we're giving to them and be able to compare and contrast what's been given with other companies. So when we think about the financial statements, then we know exactly what to expect for the most part, because it's regulated.

We have a standardized format and we have to have that standardized format in order to make these comparisons, in order to make trade and investment and transactions as easy as possible. Managerial accounting, however, is not limited in the same way. Why? Because we're not giving these reports to anybody outside the company. Their internal reports are their inner work in trying to make the internal decisions. So we might be making reports about a small group or small unit. We might be making reports about some type of product or something like that, one product out of many.

In order to make those types of decisions, we could format the reports in any way we want because we're not giving them to external users who are then relying on them to make decisions. So we have a lot more flexibility for that reason, for managerial accounting to run reports, to make reports, to think about, you know, what, what can we do in order to to make the best decisions? And what kind of data do we need in order to do that?

The availability of the data, financial accounting is typically going to be if it's a publicly traded company in particular, it's going to go through an audit. We're not going to have the data possibly quarterly or yearly. We have to wait through that audit process to take place for them to really be finalized, to have those financial statements. So it could be a very set process on when we're going to get those numbers. And the numbers might not be finalized, Of course, for a little bit of time after, you know, after the period has ended. Whereas managerial accounting and that, Of course, deals with regulations.

We have to go through the regulations. We have to make sure that everything is set up in accordance with rules and regulations, especially if it's a publicly traded company. Do these financial statements align with generally accepted accounting principles and whatnot? That process is going to take time for financial accounting, and it's very regulated for managerial accounting. We don't have that same kind of regulation. We have limits, Of course, but those limits are typically going to be what can we do? So for managerial accounting, the question is often a cost benefit analysis. You know, we could get this more information.

The question is, is it worth it for us to get more information? There's always a balancing question of is it worth us to put in the time to get more detailed information? Or is the better decision that we can probably make with that more detailed information not worth the added cost? That's typically the type of decision making restraints that we have on managerial accounting as opposed to the types of regulatory restraints. So if we want to put numbers together, if we want to put reports together, if we want to analyze whatever we want to analyze internally, no problem, except that it costs money to do so.

And we want to make a cost benefit analysis to decide whether or not the time spent is worth the effort as opposed to conforming to regulations as is typically going to be what we're going to do with financial accounting. The time focus for financial accounting is typically going to be our past. We're looking into the past. In other words, we're looking at historical data. Now, Of course, investors have and are going to be looking to project into the future as well. But all the financial statement preparation is geared towards what happened in the past from our side, from putting the stuff together from the company side.

We're trying to just say, hey, what happened? And put it together as accurately as possible. And then the investors could make future projections based on that managerial accounting. When we put this information together, it usually has a future focus. So we're trying to focus on future decision making. So when we put together reports, internal reports, whatever we need to do from an internal standpoint, we're typically thinking about what we can do for the future in this place so that we can increase production? If we look at the information focus, it's going to be on the entire organization for financial accounting.

We're looking for information that's going to affect the entire organization, and that's by design. The financial statements are there for the entire organization because investors and creditors are typically worried about the entire organization. They're not really looking into the details. They're not looking at segments of the organization. Well, and but for the most part, I think the reporting is going to give a whole as a whole what things look like as an entire on a managerial accounting. We're more typically going to go more into detail.

We're going to look at the department by department. We're going to look at product by product and try to make those decisions. So typically, financial accounting is looking at the big picture. How do we stand overall, whereas managerial accounting is going to go down into more of the nitty gritty and try to figure out what we can do from a piece by piece standpoint to improve operations, nature of information, and financial accounting is going to be purely monetary. So remember that Of course, the balance sheet is going to have things like equipment on it and this stuff and stuff that's not money in and of itself.

Equipment is equipped, could be a forklift or something, but when we put on the financial statement, we report it in terms of dollars. Everything is reported in terms of dollars. And Of course, that same information will be used in managerial accounting. But it's not the only type of information we recognize that that's only one set of information. If we can put numbers to something, we typically will, because that makes things a lot easier to compare and contrast if we have numbers to them. But oftentimes we may not have numbers. The numbers may not be representing monetary amounts.

We might be having to compare other types of things, time or other types of things. And we could have other things that are completely non numeric that we're comparing. We might have to actually compare different types of data, actually just reviews or something like that and try to make managerial decision making processes based on that. So again, we typically will break things down to a monetary basis if possible, break things down to a numeric basis if possible, because that's better for making comparisons or easier to make comparisons. But we're also going to use any type of data that we can to increase decision making processes.

Cost Classifications

Within the cost classifications chapter of the Book. We'll talk about different ways that costs can be classified in managerial accounting. Cost classifications are going to be important within managerial accounting because we often want to group costs in different formats depending on the types of information we want to get for the decisions that we are making.

For example, we may want to classify their costs by behavior. We also might want to classify costs by the function, what the costs are used for. We'll use these terms of cost classifications within a job cost system as we track the costs related to inventory through the process, from raw materials to work in process and finally to the finished product to finished goods inventory and then through the sale to cost of goods sold.

Cost Classifications Part 2

In this chapter, we will take a look at cost classifications. There's a few different ways that we can classify costs, and they all have their pros and cons. There are benefits to classification in different ways. We're going to classify costs here by behavior. Now, you may think, what does that mean? Do costs have behavior? And we could say, well, yeah, costs do have behavior in that they act in certain ways in relation to other activities.

We're going to classify the two types of costs here being fixed costs and variable costs. This type of classification is not included in financial accounting. So if you're going from financial accounting to managerial accounting, this is going to be a new concept. And the reason we're going to have cost classifications by behavior is that it really helps with projection. So we have to have this because when we're looking into the future, what's really going to be helpful if we can determine how costs act so that we can make projections based on different levels of production? So we have fixed costs.

Fixed costs mean that as production level rises, the cost remains fixed. So, for example, if we have the activity down here, we'll say this is production. If we're making units of something, as we make more units of something, the cost total remains the same. Remember here that we're talking about total cost, not cost per unit. We're starting here with total cost. So, for example, if we're saying that the rent is going to be $1,000 a month, then it really doesn't matter how many units we make.

If we're producing things in a warehouse and we make one unit in that warehouse, then it still costs $1,000. If we are producing in that warehouse and we make, say, 100 things, the rent still is $1,000. If we keep producing in that warehouse and we maximize the production in the warehouse, let's say it's 5000 things. Well, then units of production, whatever we make, then it's still going to cost us $1,000. No matter what we do, the rent is going to be the same. And so if you look at that in terms of the fixed costs, you're going to say, well, it's going to be what it is no matter what.

So when making projections, then we can think of, okay, how many units do we have to produce in order to pay off the rent, pay off the fixed cost? So the other types of behavior that we're going to have, the major second group that we're going to have for, we're going to try to basically break everything out into these two groups, even though it's not possible or not, all costs fit nicely into these two groups. We would really like it if they did because that would simplify the world here and we're going to try to do so so that we can make accurate projections.

And so the other type is variable costs, and variable costs are going to go up with each new unit of production. So, for example, if we're making guitars and this is the cost of wood, the total cost of wood, and this is the activity, how many guitars we're going to make? Well, if we make one guitar, then it's going to cost. Or if we make one guitar here, it's going to cost so much. And then if we make two guitars, well, the activity went up and that cost is going to go up in proportion. It's going to be a straight line because the cost is going to go up with the same number of units.

Let's say the cost is for wood that's going to go in the guitar. If we make three guitars, well then the cost of wood is going to go up in proportion to the number of guitars that we're making. So it's wood or direct material that goes into the cost of production that is going to go up. You would at a constant rate and as opposed to something that is fixed, such as the rent, if we know those two things, then it's really useful for us to then make projections into the future because now we can say, okay, how many guitars do we need to make in order to, you know, get to this level of cost?

And Of course, we'll add into this pretty soon. We'll add into it the amount of revenue per guitar we're going to get. And if we take the revenue minus the variable cost, then we can say, okay, how much are we making over the variable cost to see how many units we then need to have in order to clear the rent price? And that's how we start to kind of think about these things. What do we need to produce in order to clear our costs? It's a lot easier to make those types of production projections if we can break all costs up by behavior between fixed costs and variable costs.

Now some costs will line up in these two very easily and it won't be a problem if we're talking about wood in the guitar, then that's probably pretty straightforward. If we're talking about the rent, that's pretty straightforward. But we're going to have some things that aren't quite as easy to go into. These two components they may have. Some combination between fixed costs and variable cost. And what we really want to do is break them out between those two for our projection purposes, and we'll talk about different methods that we can do that.

That's going to be one of our goals in managerial accounting is to break everything out between fixed costs and variable costs that allows us to make nice projections into the future.

Another way that we can classify costs is by function. What does that cost do? Why are we incurring this cost? So we can have indirect costs and indirect costs. Direct costs are going to be costs that are traceable to a cost object. So if we're in a production cycle, the indirect costs would be things like direct materials and direct labor. These are things that we can trace to a particular unit of inventory that we are producing. So direct materials, we know exactly if we're making guitars, for example, we can trace the wood in the guitar to a particular guitar that we are producing and allocate the cost of that wood to that piece of inventory, to that guitar.

If we're talking about direct labor, same thing. If someone is putting together a guitar, we can allocate the cost of the labor that's being put together to a particular piece of inventory, a particular guitar. On the other hand, indirect costs are things that we can't trace are not traceable to a cost to object. So examples of that are going to be maintenance costs for multiple departments or things like glue or things that we can't put to a particular guitar. If we're making one guitar, then we can't really have these indirect costs allocated specifically to that guitar.

It's going to be indirect. So if we talk about maintenance for multiple departments, then possibly the maintenance is going to be for the entire warehouse. And we can't apply the maintenance, for example, to one particular guitar because we don't know how much to apply to a particular guitar. The production process needs maintenance within the warehouse, but we can't assign it directly to a particular guitar and we can take that concept to different departments as well. If we pay for maintenance for multiple departments, then the maintenance is there for multiple departments.

But it's difficult to allocate to a particular department and we're gonna have to figure out some type of way to allocate these indirect costs. That's going to be one of the challenges we have if we have maintenance for multiple departments or multiple units of inventory. How then can we take this information and allocate it to a particular unit, a particular unit which we don't really know. We have a similar problem. If we're talking about small materials like glue or something for a guitar, it might be possible for us to to classify glue as a direct material that we can then allocate specifically to a particular guitar that was used.

It was used in. However, doing so would typically not be cost effective. So if we're talking about something like glue or something like that, then we might have to use some other type of allocation method. We don't know exactly which piece of unit of inventory it was used on. So it's indirect. So we have to find some way. Then our challenge will be to take these indirect costs, these costs that we know need to be allocated in some way in order for us to properly value our inventory and try to allocate them in some way, even though we don't know directly where they apply. And that'll typically be the concept of overhead.

So anything, for example, in a factory that we work on will be well, if we can't apply it to directly direct materials or labor, it's probably going to be an indirect cost, something that's going to go into overhead that we're then going to have to figure out how can we allocate this to our units of inventory to properly allocate the inventory. So if we're talking about depreciation on our warehouse, then that depreciation is part of the cost of making stuff, making the guitars. But how do we allocate to any particular guitar?

We're going have to figure out how we can make those types of allocations. There's a supervisor in the set and in the warehouse that's supervising all the guitars we make. How do we know how much time we should put that supervisor's time on a particular job? We'll have to figure out how we can make those allocations. So that's going to be one of the challenges we'll have as we work through the manufacturing process, as we allocate costs.

Product Costs & Period Costs

In this chapter, we will take a look at product costs and period costs. When considering a manufacturing company, we can break out the costs to those costs that are used to create the product, to create the inventory, the inventory that we will eventually sell and those that will not. The product costs are going to include costs of direct labor, direct material and overhead. So we just want to memorize these types of things.

As to the three main categories we will be using when we manufacture inventory, when we make the asset of inventory, when we make the stuff that we're going to sell, that stuff is not just stuff meaning not just direct materials. In other words, a creation of something like a guitar that we intend to sell is not composed of just the materials in the guitar, the wood, the strings and whatnot, but it's substantially composed of other things such as labor and overhead. So these are the three things that make up the cost of the guitar that we're going to sell, make up the cost of whatever product it is that we sell.

The direct materials are pretty straightforward. This is going to be the material that goes directly into the units of inventory that we're creating. So for creating guitars, for making guitars, the wood is clearly a direct material that we can assign specifically to inventory and more specifically to whatever batch of inventory, whatever unit of guitar that we are making. The direct labor is very similar in that we are applying labor directly to a unit of production. So if we're making guitars and we have a custom guitar, let's say, and an individual producing that guitar, then the labor that's being put in will be included in that guitar.

And again, it's a little bit less conceptual to think about that the labor is being included in the guitar, it's not physically in the guitar, it's something that's intangible within the guitar. But when we think about the cost of the guitar, it's far more than just the wood that's in the guitar. The cost is primarily the labor that's going to be in the guitar, the thing that converts that wood into something useful, a guitar. So that's going to be the direct labor that we can apply directly. And then we have this bucket of overhead, the most confusing bucket, the bucket we're going to have to do something about, something with, and those are going to be things that we cannot apply directly to a specific unit. So if we're in a specific area.

So for example, if we're making guitars and we're applying costs directly to a guitar, if we make custom guitars, then things that we can't apply directly might be things like glue because it's so small that we don't want to apply it directly would take too much time for us to to apply out the glue to the guitar, so to track the amount of glue we use and whatnot. So what we'll do is we'll put it in the overhead and then we'll find some type of cost allocation to then allocate it out. And that's going to include anything that we can't allocate directly. So if we think about things like overhead in the factory, anything within the factory that we use that we cannot apply directly pretty much anything other than direct materials or direct labor, things like the depreciation on the factory.

We're going to have to apply that out to the guitars. We need the factory to make the guitars. If we weren't making guitars, we wouldn't have the factory and therefore wouldn't be depreciating it. And so the cost of that depreciation should be allocated to the guitars, but we want to allocate it specifically to units of guitars if we're using a job cost system. Things like a supervisor salary. We don't know who the supervisor was supervising at any given time or how much time was spent supervising one job versus another job.

And therefore, we're going to have to allocate that production supervisor to overhead and then figure out some type of allocation method. So the utilities on the factory are the same way, maintenance on the factory. So we're going to have this is going to be the most challenging of our segments here. So we know it's part of production. That's not a problem. Anything in the factories, part of production. But it becomes challenging to note if we're in a job because of our process cost, what job or what process should this overhead go to? And then we're going to have period costs.

Now the period costs are typically you can think of them as things that are not going to be part of the production, part of the inventory. These costs up here, direct labor, direct materials and overhead are going to be costs. The production costs are going to be the cost that we're going to use to create the product. And therefore, they're going to be capitalized when we use them. And this missile seems a little unusual if you're used to looking at a service company, because when we do something like pay wages, for example, we're not used to we're pretty much used to just saying it's going to be a wage expense. And here we're going to put it as part of the inventory asset.

When we use materials, we might think of it as a materials expense. We're going to capitalize it as an asset when we do things such as overhead depreciation and things like that. We're used to saying depreciation, expense and expense, but here we're going to capitalize it because it's part of the product that we're going to make. When are we going to expense it? When we sell the product.

The period costs, on the other hand, are going to be costs that are not related to the production of the product, and they're going to act more typically, as we would think when we're dealing with like a service type company, they're going to be costs for a particular time period and they're typically broken out between two items selling and administrative, and they act like we would think for a service type company. So if we're talking about the executive salary, anything that's not in the warehouse, anything that's not in the production area, which will be very distinct and like a book problem, we'd have to separate that and separate what's in production and what's not.

If we're talking about the corporate office that's not in production, anything in there will probably act very similar to a service company. Meaning if we pay the salary of administrative staff or the accounting staff, then that's going to be done during the period because the cost was incurred during that period. We paid people in order to do the job during that time period. The matching principle would then allow us to expense it at the point in time that basically the wages happened.

For the most part, the utilities on the executive office, unlike the utilities on the production on the factory, which would go into overhead if it was a utilities bill on the executive office, we would expense it like we would typically think if we're talking about depreciation. If it was depreciation on the Executive Office, we would depreciate the expense. If it was in the factory, we would include it in the inventory in some way.

So these selling and administrative expenses are typically going to act a little bit more like we would think if we're used to having dealt with companies that aren't production, companies that don't deal with making inventory, companies that either buy or sell inventory, or companies that are service companies, as you would imagine that most of our time here is going to be up here in the production cost to make the product one, because that's the most interesting part because that's where we have to all the activities happening within a manufacturing company that we have to track all this stuff and do because that's going to be something that's different than other types of of industries.

Therefore, that's where we want to focus our time. If we look at some examples of the type of classifications that we've had so far, we had variable cost versus fixed cost, direct or indirect cost and product or period costs. So if we think let's look at some examples and think about where they would go in these cost allocations. And again, when we first learn this stuff, some people probably learn a few of these allocations better than others. It's important for us to know all of them. So the variable costs versus fixed cost, the behavior that we're going to have between the cost of direct or indirect, can we apply the cost out to a particular unit, a particular function and a product costs or period cost really is dealing with are we dealing with the inventory stuff that and that's making the inventory or are we dealing with non inventory stuff which is basically admin, administrative and selling?

So let's take a look at wood. We're going to make guitars up here. So if we have wood and there's a wood guitar, you. Say here. So I have the word guitar. We would say it's typically going to be variable because every time we make a new guitar, we're going to have to have a fixed number of increases in cost, you would think. And so that's going to be a variable cost as opposed to fixed. It's going to be direct typically because if we're making custom guitars, we would know exactly which guitar that would go to.

We would be able to assign the guitar out directly and the product or period. It's going to be clearly a product cost because the wood is going to be for the production of the guitar. If we have direct wages, someone actually making the guitar, we're paying someone to make the guitar. It once again will be variable because if we make two guitars, we would expect the wages to go up at some variable rate. If we have a direct or indirect, we're going to say it's direct because that person, we can apply their cost directly to whatever guitars they work on and in the product or period. It's clearly a product cost because we're working on the production, the cost of those wages.

And again, that's something different because then when we actually record the journal entry and we say instead of wages expense, we're going to debit the guitar. We're going to debit like work and process inventory at some time. We'll talk more about that later. And then that's going to be unusual at first because a lot of times when we go through just memorizing transactions, we think of wages as an expense just automatically without knowing the rule so much or applying the rule. Same with utilities, we're going to have utilities, not utilities expense the debit, but go into some type of asset for the inventory. That's going to feel unusual.

If we've just memorized the rule saying that utilities are always utilities expense and debit and we credit cash. So these things, it makes sense right here. But as we record, the journal entries will have to really think about it probably in order and possibly unlearn some rules advertising that's going to be typically fixed. Oftentimes it's going to be fixed advertising or is it going to be direct or indirect? It's going to be indirect.

Now, these are going to be things. Advertising isn't dealing with production, so it's not within the production. So when we think about direct or indirect, oftentimes we're thinking about the production process. Is this something that we can assign directly to a particular guitar, for example, or or is it something that I don't know which guitar was worked on? If it's selling an ad man, it may not be, sometimes you might think, well, that's not applicable. That's not as applicable because we're not really even dealing with production at all.

This is going to be as we see a period of costs. So here you could put like in a or not that is applicable or indirect. And it's going to be a period cost, meaning it's not part of the production process. It's going to be something that we pay for selling and admin. And then we have manager salaries. So manager salary, we're going to say it's fixed. We're going to say it's going to be because they get paid salary and not wages as we produce guitars, it's going to be indirect. If they're managing the warehouse, then again, we don't even know which guitar they're actually managing. They're, you know, so we're going to apply their cost out to the guitars in some format.

And we're going to say it's a product cost because we're going to say they're managing the warehouse. So this is going to be a fixed cost as opposed to what we would think that the workers of the guitar would probably be variable. We're going to say this was an hourly wage, it's indirect even though they're in the warehouse, because we don't know which guitar they're working on. We don't know who they're supervising, but we're going have to allocate that somehow. It's going to be a product cost because they are in the warehouse. So we're going have to allocate it out somehow.

Admin equipment depreciation. So if we talk about the depression depreciation for the administrative office, like the fax machines or something like the coffee machines or something like that, where depreciation is in the administrative office, not the factory. We're going to say it's fixed depreciation. We know exactly what it's going to be. It's going to be indirect or not applicable because it's not in the production, it's not in the warehouse, it's not going to the making of the product. And then it's going to be a period cost because it's in the admin, it's, it's, it's in the administrative office and therefore it's not part of production. So it's not going to be in the, in the production area. And then we have factory depreciation and factory depreciation on this type. It's both depreciation here. But notice if it's in the factory, it's still going to be fixed because we know exactly what the depreciation will be.

You know, it's a set amount. It's still going to be indirect, not because it's not in the factory this time. However, it is in the factory, meaning it should go into the production of our guitars, but we don't know which guitar it's going to go to. We made all the guitars in the factory. So how, if we have a job cost system, how do we apply it to a job to process the cost system? How do we apply it to a process? And so it's going to be a product cost. So it does apply to the product, but it is indirect because I don't know which product exactly. It goes to something like glue that we've used to make to put the guitar together.

It's going to be variable because it changes. With the number of units of guitar. We're going to need more glue with more guitars. It's going to be indirect, however, because we don't really know how much glue we used on one particular guitar, so we don't know. We can estimate it and that's what we'll have to do, but we don't know exactly what that estimate should be. And then it's going to be a product cost, so it's going to be part of the production process. So the idea here on glue is it's going to be pretty small compared to something like the wood.

So if you compare the glue and the wood up here, then we're going to say, well, the wood is variable, but it's direct because I can I can assign you know, I probably had to assign the wood that I that I took out to a particular job, whereas the glue down here is, is variable, but it's not direct because I probably didn't have to go assign out the to get the glue. I just went and got the glue. I didn't have to get any kind of documentation telling me how much glue I'm going to get to put to a particular job.

It wouldn't be worth our time to track that, and therefore it's going to be an indirect cost that we're just going to have to take that glue, whatever we are paid for the glue overall and allocate it using some kind of allocation method sales commission. So a commission on the sales, it's variable which is unusual for a period costs. So this is a period cost that would be variable. It's going to be indirect or not applicable because it's not part of the production process and it's going to be a period cost. So this is one of those costs which are a little bit confusing because at most period costs are oftentimes fixed.

So most salaries are fixed in the corporate office. We don't typically have a lot of variable cost with the sales except for the commission here. And when we do our different types of allocations, that's going to kind of how we deal with that? We're going to have to deal with that. When we think of something like projections, we're going to have to break this out to a variable cost. And in that format, it'll probably be grouped more with some of the production costs because we're trying to break out variable versus fixed.

Oftentimes when we're looking at productions, when projections that is. So sales commissions are variable, it's indirect or not applicable. And it's a period cost because it doesn't deal with the production process.

Prime Costs & Conversion Costs

In this chapter, we will take a look at prime costs and conversion costs when considering prime costs and conversion costs. We are looking at the cost of production. We're looking at production costs as opposed to period costs. When considering production costs, we always think about direct materials, direct labor and overhead.

They should always come to mind when we think about production. Any time we think about inventory, whether we make it or whether it be made someplace else, it's costs include the direct materials, direct labor overhead we are talking about a manufacturing company are going to apply these three items at this point in time because we are the individuals or the company that is manufacturing the product. So remember, it's not just the materials within the product that's one component, but the other component is going to be the labor that we're going to put into it.

The cost of the labor, the wages we pay are not going to be a period experience but be part of the cost of inventory to be capitalized, be put on the balance sheet until we sell the inventory, put on the balance sheet as a piece of the inventory as an asset. And then the overhead of anything dealing with the factory, anything that deals with the factory will be part of the inventory. If we have depreciation on the factory, if we have maintenance on the factory, if we've got supervisors within the factory that are paid salary, all that stuff is going to be in the inventory in some way. They're going to be part of the product.

So any time we think of inventory, we have direct materials, direct labor and overhead.

Now when we consider these in terms of prime costs and conversion costs, there's a bit of an overlap here because the prime costs represent what is going to be directly within the product. Therefore, the prime costs include the direct materials and the direct labor. Now the direct labor we can't really see within the product Of course, like the direct materials, but it's so closely associated with the product, it's so essential to the production that we're going to call those the prime costs. Now that's going to differentiate from conversion costs, although there are some overlaps. The conversion costs are the cost that we're going to have that will be used to convert the raw material to the finished goods. The cost. It means that we're doing something, we're doing something to the raw material.

So in the example of the guitar, the direct material would be something like the wood, the conversion would be anything we do to that in order to make it into a guitar. So conversion costs are then going to include direct labor and the overhead because the direct labor is going to be part of us processing it and the overhead is going to be included, anything that's in the factory, because Of course we need that factory in order to convert. So anything like the depreciation on the factory, the supervisor salary on the factory, the small tools that we use, the glue that we're going to use, all that stuff is part of the conversion process, part of the things that we're doing to adding on to that piece of wood in order to convert it from just a piece of wood to the end product to the guitar.

Now this is going to be an added category that we can start to get confused with something like direct versus an indirect cost. It's a bit different of a concept. We need to keep these separated. So the prime costs and the conversion costs, we're often going to use more. When we use a process cost system, we'll talk about a job cost versus a process cost system, but it's different from the direct costs and the indirect costs. Remember that our direct costs are going to be those that are direct materials and direct labor are both direct costs, which happens to be the two prime costs as well, but for different reasons. These two are going to be direct costs because we can apply those activities to a particular unit. If we have a job cost system, we can apply those two activities to a particular guitar.

We know which guitars were worked on and can therefore apply these costs to that guitar. Whereas the overhead was indirect because we didn't know which in a job cost system we wouldn't know which guitar to apply all the stuff in overhead to. We have to find some way to do that. So if you compare the two, the prime costs are utilizing the same factors as indirect costs, but for different reasons. The prime cost, meaning that they're going to be prime, the prime factors of production, the primary expenditures, the ones that are going to be most associated with the manufacturing of the inventory. So those two are similar.

The difference, Of course, is that the conversion cost is not equivalent is not at all to the indirect costs. The indirect costs are just going to be the overhead because we can't apply them. If you think of job costs and we can't apply them to the job, that's why they're indirect. That's why they're overhead. From a conversion standpoint, the conversion means anything that we're doing to the inventory to convert it. So that's why it's going to include that direct labor. So here's where the overlap is.

The direct labor becomes a bit confusing because it's both a prime cost and a conversion cost. And when we consider that and compare and contrast it to direct versus indirect, prime costs and costs happen to have the same two components, but for different reasons. The conversion is not the same as the indirect cost, because the conversion represents us converting this information, which will include this direct labor as well as the overhead.

Manufacturer's Financial Statements

Within the Manufacturers Financial Statements chapter of the Book. We'll talk about financial statements related to a manufacturing company. As we do so, we're comparing and contrasting it to other types of companies, including a service company, one that doesn't have inventory or a merchandising company, one that purchases and then sells inventory.

The manufacturer, Of course, will be producing inventory. So we'll take a look at the differences, focusing in on what will be different from a manufacturing company, that being typically things that are going to be within the production process, tracking the costs through the inventory process, through the raw materials to us, working on the raw materials to those materials being completed finished goods and finally to us selling those finished goods inventory and recording the costs on the income statement in the form of cost of goods sold.

Manufacturer's Balance Sheet

In his chapter. We will take a look at some of the differences within the balance sheet for a manufacturer, a company that produces inventory compared to a company that just purchases and sells inventory or a service company. And clearly, the difference is going to be related to inventory. So the major difference for a manufacturer's balance sheet to a service company, for example, would be that we're going to have inventory on the balance sheet. That inventory will be reported as an asset on the balance sheet, typically a current asset.

Now when we go from a company that just purchases and sells inventory to a company that actually manufactures, produces, makes the inventory, then the inventory could be broken out to components. We're going to have raw materials inventory. We're going to have to process inventory. We're going to have a finished goods inventory. Now, these may be grouped on the balance sheet in different ways within inventory, be broken out into subcategories of raw materials, work in process or finished goods, or be consolidated in some way. But we're going to have to contend with these components of inventory as we go through the production process.

These are going to be balance sheet accounts that we're going to have to track and work through as we track the inventory. You can imagine the physical flow of the inventory going through these inventory cycles. So if we make inventory, for example, we're going to have raw materials. If we make guitars, those raw materials would then be things like the wood for the guitar.

The wood would then be transferred to the work in process. Work in process is still inventory, but we can't sell it yet because it's in process. So this is the inventory that we're making.

The wood has started to be converted to a guitar, but it's not there yet. It still has value, it's still inventory. But Of course, these two components of inventory are things that we cannot yet sell within work. You can also imagine not just the raw materials as we see here, but we're going to include other things in that work in process, which is going to include the direct labor and the overhead. So as you think of these three components of inventory, it's often easy to start to think, well, the raw material went here and then it changed to work in process.

And then we finished it and went to the finished goods. As we go through that process, we're going to emphasize the fact that it's not just the raw materials that are being here and working in the process. It's going to include the direct labor and the overhead within that process, and then that's going to be converted to the finished goods. So once we're done, then we can sell the guitar. It's ready to be sold. We can put it on the market here.

It will be within finished goods that we can then sell after it's sold. Then Of course it can move to the cost of goods sold on the income statement, as we would for a normal type of company, the merchandising company that would just purchase and sell goods. So once it's in the finished goods state, then we're in a similar state as we would be for a merchandiser ready to sell that. The next step, Of course, would be that sale.

The next step would be us recording the expense in the form of cost of goods sold.

Manufacturer's Income Statement

In this chapter, we will take a look at some of the components of a manufacturer's income statement comparing and contrasting where a manufacturer's income statement may differ from a service company or a merchandiser, where a manufacturer, a company that makes the inventory could differ from a service company that has no inventory or a merchandiser who just purchases and sells inventory rather than making the inventory. Part of that will be the calculation of the cost of goods sold.

So clearly one of the differences we're going to have from a manufacturer to a service company will be related to inventory. And the major difference between the inventory accounts on the income statement is the cost of the inventory, the expense related to the inventory at the point of sale, that being the cost of goods sold. Therefore, a service company is often going to have just a single step income statement where we group up revenue and then we group up all of expenses and we subtract out to get the net income. For a merchandiser that has inventory and a manufacturer that makes inventory, we're also going to have the cost of goods sold.

The cost of goods sold will be very similar, but it will have some differences that we want to note from a merchandiser company to a manufacturing company. Very important formula we want to just memorize. This formula will be used in many different ways. So the merchandiser company, if we thought about the merchandiser company first and then convert and say, okay, what do we need to change to go to a manufacturing company to calculate the cost of goods sold for a merchandiser? A company that just purchases and sells inventory doesn't make the inventory. The cost of goods sold calculation would be the beginning inventory. What was inventory at the start of the period, the start of the month or the year? And then we're going to add to it purchases.

We know what the purchases are because we actually paid for the inventory that we bought. And therefore there's no real estimation in terms of the purchases that's going to give us the cost of goods available for sale. That's what we could have sold during the time period. If it's a month, we could have sold this many units. How many did we sell to do that? And this is kind of a periodic calculation. And again, we can use the cost of goods calculation, whether we use a periodic system or perpetual system oftentimes. But note when the format of it is kind of more of a periodic type of format because we're saying this is the cost of goods available for sale and then we're going to subtract out ending inventory, which we can imagine. We got through a physical count.

We count the inventory at the end as we would in a periodic inventory system. And therefore, if this is the inventory we had available for sale, the inventory we could have sold and this is the inventory that we have not yet sold. The difference between those two is what we have sold on a cost basis, and that's going to be the cost of goods sold. That's going to be the expense. That's what will be reported on the income statement as an expense, the most important expense for a merchandiser or a manufacturer. The cost of the inventory that we are selling.

Now, if we look at a manufacturer, we can say, okay, how can we convert this in order to deal with a manufacturer rather than a merchandiser? We're going to have that same beginning inventory and then rather than having purchases, however, we're going to add to it the cost of goods manufactured. So we didn't purchase these goods. Obviously, we did purchase the materials, but we've we're going to have cost of goods manufactured, which is going to include what we made in terms of not just materials, but what we made in terms of the work that we put in the direct labor and the overhead that's going to be put in there.

Now, this number, you might be saying, well, where are we going to get that number? We're going to have to figure that out through our production process. And once we do that, however, this is the number that we're going to use and it's not going to be purchased. So that's where the big difference is. You can see that they're basically, you know, similar and that purchasing is obviously the activity that we had happen through our merchandiser company and the manufacturer.

What had happened is that we not only purchased materials, but we made them into inventory. So that's the cost of goods manufactured. Then we'll give us the cost of goods available for sale and then we're going to do the same. Subtract out the Indian finished goods inventory. So what has been completed in the finished goods? And that will give us our cost of goods sold. So you can see the two formulas are going to be very similar. Now note that you can use this formula not just for the calculation of cost of goods sold. I mean, if there's a book question, especially multiple choice questions will often maneuver. Things are. So that we will have to solve for different types of items here. So that's one way that a multiple choice question can be used in order to test conceptual components.

And so note that any of these components of the formula are multiple choice questions that could ask for meaning. The multiple choice question could give us beginning inventory and not be asking for big in an inventory and give us the rest of the data. What we do not want to do is try to memorize a formula to get to the beginning inventory because all we're doing is adjusting the algebra. What we want to do is write down this formula and say that, okay, we have the cost of goods sold and we can back into the beginning inventory. The same would be true for if they gave us all this information but not the cost of goods manufactured.

We're not going to rewrite another formula to figure out what the cost of goods manufactured is. We're going to use this formula and just use algebra to say, okay, this is the unknown. Now I know everything else, this is the unknown. So any question that's going to be related to any of these items could be in the inventory, Of course, as well. You want to just be able to write down this formula and then apply out whatever you need. And also note, Of course, that this is a subtotal, this is a subcategory. So sometimes you can actually if you want to simplify your algebra, then you can eliminate this item.

So beginning inventory plus cost of goods sold minus ending inventory gives us the cost of goods available for sale. And then if you do that, then they can ask for the other component, they can eliminate any one of these and ask you for that. And what you want to do is just write down this formula, okay? And say this is the unknown. I don't know that one. So now I'm going to do what I have to do to make that number right. If I know this number, then I can do what I have to do to make that number what it needs to be.

If you look at the example here, we're going to say if the beginning inventory happened to be 14,000, we're going to add to it our cost of goods manufactured. What we made, we're going to say 200,000 here. That gives us what's available, 214,000. Now, Of course, note that we're talking about dollars and this is the cost of what we made here. So we're not talking about units. We're going have to convert that into dollars. And that's a bit, you know, something that more confusing than we might first think and to do that but then we have the cost of goods available for sale and then we're going to subtract out what's still in the inventory, which we can get from typically a physical account.

Now again, this physical count is in dollars, so we have $12,000 worth and the physical count would be in units which we would have to then convert in some way to dollars. If this is the number of dollars worth of inventory we had available for sale in the month and this is how much it has not yet been sold. The difference between the two then is going to be what had been sold, which we're going to say is the cost of goods sold. This then is what will be reported on the income statement reducing growth, reducing sales by the cost of goods sold to get to gross profit and ultimately to the net income.

This is going to be our most important expense on the income statement if we are a manufacturer because it's going to be the highest cost. Typically the things that we make if we make stuff is going to be the highest cost of what we do. And therefore, we're going to break it out separately most of the time and have the sales minus the cost of goods sold, giving us that subcategory of gross profit on the income statement.

Cost Flows For a Manufacturing

Within the cost flows for a manufacturing company chapter of the Book, we will discuss cost flows for a manufacturing company, a company that produces inventory, focusing therefore on the cost of inventory, the flow of costs as it goes through the materials that are purchased to us, working on the materials to the finished goods, finally to us selling those and that cost. Then go into the income statement in the form of the cost of goods sold.

We'll focus here in more of a broad sense, not looking at a job cost system in particular, but being able to look at just what would happen in terms of inventory flows in general. There are two major systems that we could use for manufacturing companies. Those being a job cost system, the one we'll focus most on this Book and a process cost system.

We want to get some idea of both of those. So we'll have to compare and contrast them a little bit in the next chapter because in order to understand either one of them, it's easiest to do that by comparing and contrasting to the other. Either one of them, however, will have similar issues in terms of tracking the production of inventory. Meaning we're going to have the raw materials that we're going to need to convert in some way to the finished goods before we can sell them, record them at an expense at the time of sale in the form of cost of goods sold.

Manufacturing Activities Flow

In this chapter, we will take a look at the manufacturing activities at flow. We'll take a look at the costs of the manufacturing process and how they flow through the manufacturing process, how we will track and organize these costs as we go.

Remember that the major difference between the cost of goods sold calculation for a merchandiser, a company that purchases and sells inventory, and a manufacturer one that makes the inventory is going to be that a merchandiser has these purchases item where they just going to purchase the inventory and the manufacturer is going to have the cost of goods manufactured. So this number then becomes the number that we need to determine how we are going to get to this? Number four, if we talk about a merchandiser, it's very easy for us to know what the purchases are because that's what we purchase. That's pretty straightforward for the manufacturer.

However, the cost of the goods we manufacture is going to include more than just what we purchase, more than just raw material. It's going to include things such as direct labor and overhead. So we'll take a look at this in three broad categories. We'll have the materials, we'll have the production, and then we'll eventually be selling the materials we're making.

Remember that the process here is, Of course, the production of inventory, the ultimate goal to be selling it. So most of this that we're thinking about is all kind of balance sheet stuff until we get to the end when we sell it, which is going to be similar to a merchandising company where once we're at the end, we sell it, moving it from the balance sheet to the income statement in the form of cost of goods sold. So first we have the materials that we think of and the materials we can think of will run through a similar process as when we just buy and sell inventory from a merchandising company, meaning we can have the materials that's already in the warehouse.

The materials that we have from last month are still there. This month we're going to include those materials that we purchase. So we're going to add purchases to those materials and then we're going to subtract from them Indian materials. What is still there? We're going to count the materials. Those will be the Indian materials and that will give us the materials used. Now this calculation should look pretty similar to our cost of goods sold, but you want to be able to understand this calculation because it's the same kind of thing for our cost of goods sold for a merchandising company and similar to the cost of goods sold for a manufacturer as well.

We have to begin inventorying materials. We could have a subcategory if we wanted to obtain materials available for use. And then we're going to subtract out the Indian materials to give us the materials used. So this is going to be our purchase. And you can think of this just as us purchasing the materials that we have and going through this process to determine the materials that we're going to use within production. Now, once that happens, we're going to say, okay, that's going to go to our production area here. This number here is going to be part of production. This is what we used to produce, but it's not the only thing that we had in production because in production we also had the beginning work in process.

When we think about production, we're thinking about what's in process work and process wipe. Whip is often used here. So we're going to say, well, we already had some stuff that was in process now and this month, according to this calculation, we included more materials here based on this calculation to the work in process. And so we're going to add that in, but we're also going to add direct labor and overhead. And these are the two areas that are often overlooked within the production process, because when we think of goods and services, we often think of just the stuff it's made out of.

It's made out of plastic, it's made up there, guitars made out of wood. But Of course, the major components that comprise the cost of it are labor and overhead. So we have to include that in the production process. And these two items are the confusing things to most people because they're going to differ when we record them here as to when we had a service company or a company that just buys and sells inventory because some things like utilities on the warehouse, some things like depreciation, we're not going to expense them as we had in the past. We're going to include them in the cost of production.

We're going to include them in the cost of inventory. And that's then we're going to subtract out the ending work and process what's still there, what's not completed yet. So we're going to count what's still in the process and not yet done, and that'll give us the cost of goods manufactured. So again, these two calculations you can see of them are similar. They're similar in nature, meaning we had beginning work in process and then not purchases, but the materials used and all the labor, these three items being what we added to it, what we made from it.

We didn't buy it, we made it, we transferred over this and then we added the labor and overhead. Those are all costs that we have. What? Into it. We could have been beginning. We could then have a subcategory if we chose to, which would be work in process available and then and then subtract out the ending work in process. So it's similar to the formulas that we have here. This time our bottom line numbers are getting to the cost of goods manufactured, not to be confused with the cost of goods sold. Cost of goods manufactured is what we made during this time period.

Cost of goods sold is going to be what we actually sold during this time period. Cost of goods manufactured will be used in the calculation for the cost of goods sold. However, that would be the beginning inventory. I'm sorry, beginning the finished goods inventory. So now we're looking at the goods that are done now in the finished goods inventory and then we're going to add to it the cost of goods manufactured instead of, as we would for a merchandiser, a company that just purchases and sells inventory where this would be purchased. So this is the different number here between those two that's going to give us the goods available for sale. Just a subcategory. This is what we could have sold during the time period. This is our calculation of the cost of goods sold that we saw prior.

And then that's going to give us our Indian finished goods and then we're going to subtract from that our Indian finished goods inventory, which we could get from a physical account to finally get the cost of goods sold. Now, notice we have the sales item here. The only area here that's going to be on the income statement is the cost of goods sold. And it's not a sale item. We don't know what we sold it for. But this flow doesn't track the sales price.

The sales price has nothing to do directly with the cost of goods sold. We might use the cost to derive the sales price. But remember we're tracking the cost. So when we sell something, we're going to if it's a perpetual system, we're going to debit cash or debit accounts receivable, credit sales revenue sales will be recorded. That's the part that's not here. We're also going to debit the cost of goods, sell the expense and reduce inventory. And that's in credit inventory and that's what we are tracking here. This is going to be the cost of goods sold, the expense portion of the sales that we make.

When we make a sale, we have the related expense of the cost of goods sold. Note that this expense, this one time that we're finally hitting the income statement, consists of all this activity that we've done. The direct materials are included in it, the direct labor is included in it, the overhead is included in it. All that stuff that we've been tracking this whole time and haven't been put in on the income statement at all. We've just been putting it on the balance sheet as just lumping it in together as part of inventory is finally being expensed all together as we sell it in the form of cost of goods sold.

Just In Time (JIT) Manufacturing

In this chapter, we will take a look at the manufacturing concept of a just in time inventory system. The concept of a just in time inventory system is going to be that we're going to start to put together the inventory after we get the order. In other words, we're going to get an order from the customer and then start to put together the inventory. For example, if we're a Dell computer and we're putting together computers, we're going to get the order for the computer before we start to assemble it. There are pros and cons to a just in time system.

One of the pros is it's often considered to be more customer focused because we can allow for the customer to give us a bit more customization if we're going to create and put together the computer after it has been ordered. It's also helpful that we may not have to have as much cost and just inventory being stored. If we're able to just create these computers as we go, we don't have it. We don't need as much warehouse space. We don't need to just be storing computers.

We don't need to deal with the risk of those computers that have already been assembled to go down in value and no longer be desirable in the market. We can just build them as we go. So the concept is we're going to get the customer order and then we're going to schedule production at that point in time. Notice this has to happen pretty quickly. We needed it because we wanted to get the computer out pretty quickly. So all these components of production then are going to have to happen smoothly. And that's going to be one of the downfalls.

Of course, if there's any problems with any of these processes along the way to the production of the computer, then we don't we don't have any warehouse in order to just go and pick up a computer. So that's going to be one of the risks that we have. Then we're going to get the materials just in time for production. We're going to go ahead and get the materials. That means we have to have a good relationship with our suppliers and make sure that we can get everything we need at the point in time of order.

And as long as these things are all secure, then a just in time system can the benefits outweigh the cost? And then we want to complete it just in time for assembly. So we're going to complete the parts so that we can assemble it. And then we're going to complete products just in time to ship. So notice all these things are basically happening very quickly after the customer has made an order and all of these lengths along the way for it to work will need to have good communication with our suppliers.

We need to be able to assemble everything in a systematic process and have everything done fairly quickly. If that's the case, then we have the benefit of being able to have a more customer centered design so that we can have some more flexibility in the types of products we're going to put together. And that's generally going to be beneficial and what our customers are looking for oftentimes these days.

Job Cost vs Process Cost System

Within the job cost versus process cost system chapter of the Book, we will compare and contrast a job cost system and a process cost system. The two major systems that we can use in a manufacturing company for a company that produces inventory.

This Book will be focusing on a job cost system. But in order to understand the job cost system fully, we need to compare and contrast it to the alternative, the other type of system that could be used, and that would be the process cost system.

Job Cost Vs Process Cost

In this chapter, we will compare a job cost and process cost system. When we produce inventory, when we are a manufacturing company, we typically will be using either a job cost system or a process cost system. And the difference between these two? Which one we will use will typically depend on the type of inventory that we produce. So let's go through the characteristics that will generally be apparent or be present when we use a job cost system. And when we look at these, we want to compare and contrast the two.

When would we use the job cost system? When would we use a process cost system? As we start to work through problems of the job cost system and the process cost system, we'll start to see why these characteristics of inventory are going to be those that will distinguish whether we choose to be a job cost system or a process cost system. For now, just note that a job cost system means that we're going to apply the cost of the inventory to particular jobs. So we're going to have a particular job. We're going to assign the costs to that job as opposed to a process cost system where we are going to assign costs to a process as we go. So as we think of this, we're going to think of the example of custom guitars.

Pretty much anything custom that you can think of, you can that's one type of thing that would basically usually be in a job cost system. So if we get an order for a guitar, it's going to be a specific type of guitar and we're going to custom make this guitar in accordance with the order. We would typically use more of a job cost system. It's also something that if you think of custom like construction and stuff like that, construction jobs are typically going to be different in nature and therefore we typically use the job cost system. So that's the first characteristic we'll have. If a custom order, then we're typically going to use a job cost system.

Now I would use that characteristic in order to then think about the other characteristics as following from it. Meaning if we do some type of manufacturing business that's custom in some way, then the other things are going to follow from if we make custom guitars, if we make any kind of construction, it's going to be custom to whatever needs to be done. Then we're typically going to be doing a job cost system. Our next characteristic are heterogeneous product products or services, and that just means that they're different. And the reason I use this word is because sometimes you'll see it in textbooks. So heterogeneous and homogeneous, heterogeneous being the opposite, meaning different and homogeneous meaning the same.

So this, Of course, follows that we can just say, Of course, that the types of things we're producing are not all exactly the same. And that follows from the idea that they're custom, they're different in some way. We've got some differences in the production that we have. And because of those differences, we cannot do things like just allocate the costs evenly to whatever we're making. If one guitar we make is a lot more detailed than another guitar we make, then we cannot evenly allocate the costs. And that's going to be one of the reasons we use the job cost system. If we do a construction job and one happens to be a lot larger than another, then we can't allocate the same cost to those two jobs. So we shouldn't, we should find some other way. And that's why we're going to use a job cost system as opposed to a process cost system.

Low production volume. Now, low production volume means that we're not producing as many of the items possible as in a job cost type of inventory system. Meaning if we're making custom guitars, then we're going to produce far less of them. That's okay, because we're going to charge a higher price for the ones that we produce, as opposed to if we were just stamping out the guitars and they're all the same, then the idea there is that we're going to have a high volume, less customization. So a job cost system follows from the idea that we're going to have some differentiation, some custom. And that means that the products are going to be different in nature.

Differences in nature of whatever we make typically would mean that the production volume will be lower. And then we're going to have high product flexibility. Again, that's going to follow from the idea that they're custom so that if something's going to be different in nature from anything that we're making, that's going to be different and we might just specialize even if we're just specializing in guitars. And even if it's fairly limited, if we have the more customization we have within that guitar, the more we're going to need to have a job cost system as opposed to a process cost. If we're in construction, Of course, we might do the same type of construction all the time, but the jobs that we go to and deal with are typically going to be different just by the nature of the job.

And so we're going to have to have differences there. They'll be flexible that we will have, basically based on the fact that they're going to be custom in some manner. Also, the job cost system will typically have higher value, higher dollar values for the products as opposed to a process cost system because and that leads through the customization. If we're going to customize it, then it's going to take more time and it's going to cost more as opposed to if it was all just being the same thing. Our goal there is to lower costs and have it be typically cheaper. So if we can contrast this to a process cost system, the idea of a process cost system is we're going to apply the costs to the process.

And the reason we can do that is because all the things that we make are going to be, in essence, the same. So that's going to be our route again that we want to think about as opposed to something being customized here. Everything is what it is. You get what you get. It's all going to be the same. So we don't need to apply the costs in the same way. We need to apply the costs all evenly to the units. So what we need to do then we can do that by using a process cost system, assigning costs as they go through the process rather than to particular units of inventory, particular jobs. So in this, I would think of something like taffy. If we're making taffy or caramel candies or something like that, they're all the same.

We're not going to vary the caramel candies. They're all the same. So we're producing our inventory. Other things like oil are going to be like that for processing oil. It's all the same at the end of the process. So our goal here is to make everything the same and lower costs. So we're going to have repetitive procedures. Everything is going to be the same. And our goal here again is just to make everything the same, even mechanized if possible, have the whole machine make the taffy and go through just the process of making the taffy. And once we automate the system because they're all the same, then that should be lowering the cost.

We're going to have homogeneous product products or services as opposed to heterogeneous products. So they're all the same. And again, this is probably the one that you want to focus on here or the fact that they're not custom. So we don't have custom products that are all going to be the same in nature and therefore everything else pretty much derives from that. We're going to have high production value. That's the point. I was making everything the same. We're going to say you have no variance. You want caramels with different kinds of things in them or whatnot. We don't do that. We just make the caramels. They're all the same and we have a pretty low cost because of that.

The more we try to customize the caramels, then the more it's going to be, you know, difficult for us to automate the process. Then we're going to have more customization. So if we keep them all the same, we can have higher production volume and lower cost low production flexibility. Again, that follows from them all being pretty much the same and not being customized. So we're not going to vary what we produce. We're going to say these are all we're all going to produce the same thing for every every unit is going to be the same. So if we look at these together, then the job costs and the process cost system remember that the job cost system has the custom order as opposed to non custom orders, which are the repetitive procedures on the process cost system.

So this site is going to be custom, this site is not custom and that means that we're going to have everything be repeated. It's just it is going to be what it is. And then we're going to have heterogeneous production from the job cost versus the process cost homogeneously. And again, this kind of falls out from the fact that these are custom and these are non custom. So these are going to be all different products and services through that customization. These will all be the same.

The job cost system, low production volume again because they're all different in nature and a high production volume for the process call system because they're all the same. We can then scale up and be able to produce a lot more than the job cost system. High product flexibility, we can vary. That's the point. At the point of having them be custom on the process cost is. Then we have no product for flexibility. And again, that's that's the point, because that's what leads us to be able to produce more at that time.

Cost Flows for a Job Cost System

Within the job cost versus process cost system chapter of the Book, we will compare and contrast a job cost system and a process cost system. The two major systems that we can use in a manufacturing company for a company that produces inventory.

This Book will be focusing on a job cost system. But in order to understand the job cost system fully, we need to compare and contrast it to the alternative, the other type of system that could be used, and that would be the process cost system.

In this chapter, we will take a look at a job cost system cost flow. We'll look at those costs flow a few different times, a few different ways. But now we want to get an overview of that cost flow. So we get an idea of where we're going. Well, then look at their cost flow as we go through a comprehensive problem. When we go through a comprehensive problem, however, we often start to look at the very specific component that we are on in a fairly long problem.

So as we do that, we want to get an idea and keep an idea in our heads of what the overall cost flow will be so that we know when we're focusing in on one particular component, how it fits into the big picture, that'll give us more context, more motivation to learn the particular step that we are looking at. So whenever we think of manufacturing costs, we want to think of materials, overhead costs and labor and just start any inventory that we think of, not just in terms of if we are the manufacturer, they include these items and it's easy to think of inventory as materials. So if we think of a TV, we think of the materials that are in the TV, but notice that a lot of that is going to be due to overhead and labor.

A lot of the costs. A lot of the value, a lot of what it is. We just took the raw materials of a TV that wouldn't amount to much unless they were put together to format a TV. So it's important to know when we do a manufacturing company, Of course, we are providing some of those products, some of that value. So we have the raw materials, we're going to have the overhead, we're going to have the labor. We're going to have to account for all three of those in the cost of whatever we make. We make a TV. We got to include all of those in the cost of the TV. We have to track all those costs so that we can include them in the cost of our inventory. How will that work then?

Well, if we start with our materials here, clearly we will buy the materials, whatever is going to be used to create our TV, the plastic and whatnot that are going to be used to create the TV. We're going to have those and that's going to be a part of inventory. And then we're going to start to work on those. And once we do that, we're going to put it into what we call work in process. So work processes are starting to convert whatever the raw materials are to the finished product, the TV. So now our materials over here are going to be taken from the materials and put into a working process as we start the job, as we start to get going with the process of making now, we want to keep in mind that this work in process, this is going to be an account called work in process.

And when we're thinking about a job cost system, we're not going to be able to apply anything to this work in process unless we can assign it to a job. So if it's within work in process, we need to have it be supported by a job. And that's going to be similar to if we had, say, an accounts receivable account. We can't apply anything to our accounts receivable account unless we also have a subsidiary ledger and a customer to apply it to. We need to know who owes us the money. Well, when we go to a job class system for work in process, it's similar. If I put these materials from the materials to the work in process account, I need to know which job that we're working on. And so that's going to be our criteria.

Now, if it's direct labor, if we're making say, let's go back to the guitars, if we're making a guitar and we're putting the wood in the guitar, we know exactly which guitar the wood's going to. On the other hand, if we're talking about some of these materials that we don't know exactly which guitar is going to things like glue, things like small components that are going to be included in the guitar. It's not worth us to track exactly which guitar they go to. We're not going to get a requisition form and say, I need this specific amount of glue to put together this guitar. It would not be cost effective to do so. So what we'll do is we'll take some of this material and we'll put it into overhead.

We can't put it up here yet. We can't put it into the working process account because we don't. We can't assign it to a particular job and nothing goes over here until we can assign it to a particular job. This overhead is also going to include any other type of overhead that we have. So when we think of overhead in general, these are all types of things that we basically spend on the warehouse where we make things. So that's going to include things like depreciation on the warehouse. If we have a supervisor salary in the warehouse, we don't know which job that they're working on. So it's going to go into overhead. If we have maintenance in the warehouse, then all of that's going to go to some inventory, but we don't know which job to assign it to, so it's going to be in there.

If we have utilities in the warehouse, it's going to be in overhead. And that overhead then Of course, is going to be a cost that will be included in overhead. Then we're going to take that overhead and we will assign it to the work in process. How will we do that? That's going to be one of the things that we'll have to figure out, because we cannot just take this overhead and assign. To work in process. We can analyze it there and put it into that account. But we need to know which job it goes to. And that's going to be one of our problems. One of the things that we'll have to figure out from this step here to assigning the overhead to a job.

We're going to have to figure out which job gets how much overhead, because some of the stars are custom guitars. Some of them are more specialized than others. It would be similar if we had a construction company. Some of them are larger companies. Some of them are smaller projects and larger projects. We need to know how much of the supervisor salary or how much of the small materials we use, how much of the truck and gas it possibly would go into each individual job when they're not all the same in size.

And we don't have any way to assign them particularly to each job. So that's going to be one of our problems that we'll talk through as we work through the job cost system, the labor. Same thing. We're going to take the labor and we're going to assign it to the work in process. And that's going to be direct labor. So any time we have someone working on a particular guitar, it's pretty easy for us to see which job, which guitar that person is working on and therefore be able to assign their cost directly to work and process and back it up by job cost sheets.

However, we may have some people working in the warehouse that we cannot assign to a particular job. And those would be things like possibly the supervisor salary, possibly the maintenance in the in the in there, because we don't know which job it goes to. And therefore, we're going to say, well, it's still labor. It's going to be labor. We're going to have payroll happening. But some of that labor is going to be directly to the job, direct labor, and some of it will be indirect. If we can't assign it directly to the job, then we're going to include it as well. And this overhead. So you can see this overhead is a big bucket of stuff that basically we cannot assign or it would be too not cost effective to assign directly to a particular job and therefore we will use some other format.

Once we have these items in work, in process, at some point in time, we are going to finish them within the work in process and we can then transfer them to the finished goods. So once we're in finished goods, then the finished goods are going to include all of these items, raw materials, overhead and labor within the job. But we're basically going to have a job that will be completed and that job will be in finished goods, will have the concept or the account of finished goods.

Note that these two accounts on the general ledger are just going to be one account on the general ledger, we're going to have work in process. But within the working process, it's made up of job cost sheets. So these are like sub ledgers that are backed up in a similar way as accounts receivable would be one account on the general ledger, but it's supported by a subsidiary ledger, breaking that information out by customer. So in this case, all of these accounts, remember, are going to be broken up or backed up, supported by a general ledger account, breaking the information out by date. But these are also going to be supported by another account, another ledger, another source document that's going to give us the information in terms of jobs. So the finished goods then are going to be one number.

We're going to transfer it from work in process to finished goods. But we will still know which jobs are going to be applied to the finished goods. And those jobs, Of course, are made up of materials overhead and labor. And then once we have the finished goods, we're kind of at the end product now. Now we can sell them. If we're talking about guitars, we can sell them now, right? So now is the final step, which is similar to a merchandising company we sell, and that will go to the cost of goods sold.

Now, as we go through this process, it's easy for us to forget about just the normal sales journal entry, because this whole process leads up to us selling the inventory. That's the point of the business. But none of this is tracking the sales price. We may use the cost sheets to derive the sales price, but the sales price is not directly related to what we're tracking here.

We're tracking the cost. So at the end of the day, the last journal entry is going to be increasing sales, credit to sales and debit the accounts receivable or cash. And none of that journal entry is not being represented here because we don't know exactly what the sales price is based on this information. What will be here is when we make a sale in a perpetual system.

The second half of that journal entry is debit to the cost of goods sold, the expense related to the sale. That's what's here. And a credit to inventory a reduction of the asset related to the sale. And Of course that cost of goods sold then is going to be the jobs that we're going to be selling, you know, a particular job that we made particular guitars or. Construction jobs. Those jobs consist of materials overhead and labor.

Accounting From Beginner to Advanced!

Get into accounting by learning these skills. Once you are done with this Book, you will be able to update your resume and begin applying for accounting jobs. This Book is better than an accounting coach.

I believe that you should not fall asleep when learning something new. You need to be encouraged and excited instead. In order to be excited about learning, you need to understand easily. I have implemented a new way of teaching. Animated videos which are easy to understand. Problem solving videos that teach you how to apply what you have learned. Learning has never been so exciting.

This Book will teach you the basics and fundamentals in Accounting in a FUN way! I Guarantee, you will not fall asleep. If you do, get your money back. No questions asked.

Included are additional problems and exercises and the appropriate explanations as well.

Compare this entire Book with an entire semester. You will be able to grasp all the concepts in financial accounting in just a few hours. Enroll!

Who this Book is for

1. CPA Exam Takers
2. Business Owners
3. Students
4. Businesses
5. Accountants
6. Bookkeepers

What is Accounting?

Welcome to chapter one. We will start our Book by learning what Accounting is. Accounting consists of three main activities. It identifies, records, and communicates economic events of an organization to interested users. What do we understand from this definition? There are three main activities, first one is identification, second one is recording, and third one is communicating.

If I want to make it easier to understand, we will consider identification as inputs, recording as the process, and finally communication as outputs. Let us start with identification and identify relevant events. What do we mean by relevant events? They have economic significance to a particular company, which any occurrence will impact the company financial condition. So, relevant events are more company specific which differ from one business to another. Such as sales of meals in a restaurant, another example is purchasing of manufacturing machines in a factory.

The second activity is recording, it includes recording economic events in systematic and chronological entries. What does Chronological mean? It means events are recorded in the order in which they happened or incurred. To record these events, they must be measured in dollar value or any other currency. During the process of recording, these events are classified in accounting ledgers. We will talk about ledgers in depth later in this Book.

One of the mistakes that people make when thinking about accounting, they always refer to it as bookkeeping. Actually, bookkeeping is the recording process only in accounting activities. Bookkeeping doesn't equal Accounting. The final activity is communicating, there are two main roles in this stage. First one is accumulating similar transactions to report them in the aggregate in financial statements. We will see this step later in this Book once we explain the accounting cycle. The second role is to analyze & interpret reported information using different methods. Such as ratios, graphs, trends and relationships. We will explain how to analyze financial statements later in this Book as well. This is the end of our chapter, thanks for reading and see you with the next one.

Users of Financial Information

We learned in our previous chapter what accounting is. Today, we will talk about users of financial information. There are two main groups of users, the first one is internal users and the second one is external users. Internal users are managers who run the business, while external users are individuals or organizations who want to know about the financial condition or the capability of the company.

Let us start with some examples of internal users. The first department is Finance. For example, they want to know whether there is sufficient funds to pay bonuses to employees or dividends to stockholders. Another example is the sales department. They want to know the best price to sell their products or services in the market. We also have a production department. They may ask what is the cost of production per unit? and how to reduce it effectively without losing quality? There is also a human resources department. They may ask can we afford providing increments to our employees this year or not?

Our last example is Management. It is important to the management to know which product line is profitable and which one is losing. For external users, let us take another example. The first user is investors. They need financial information to decide whether to buy, hold or sell their ownership shares of the company. Another user is banks. They want to evaluate the risk of providing bank facilities or lending money to the company. Another example is suppliers, to study whether to provide credit terms to the company or limit their sales to be on cash basis only.

One more example is customers. When there is a long term contract between the company and its customer, the customer uses accounting information related to the company to know about its financial capabilities to insure smooth operation during the contract period. This is more common in the construction business. The customer wants to make sure only bidders with good financial capabilities can bid and earn such contracts. The last example is the government, such as the tax authority. They want to assure compliance with laws, regulations, and tax calculations. This is the end of our chapter, thanks for reading and see you with the next one.

What is GAAP?

After we learned about users of financial information. In this chapter, we will talk about GAAP. GAAP refers to "Generally Accepted Accounting Principles". It is a common set of standards, rules, and procedures, which indicate how to report economic events in the financial statements. There are two main groups supporting establishing GAAP in the United States. The first organization is FASB. FASB refers to the Financial Accounting Standards Board, which is an independent, private sector, not-for-profit organization that establishes standards for both public & private companies.

The second group is the SEC. SEC refers to the U.S. Securities and Exchange Commission, which is a government agency that established reporting requirements for public companies, who are required to follow GAAP. SEC depends on FASB for setting the standards, they are not setting these standards themselves. By applying GAAP standards, financial statements will earn multiple benefits. We will focus here on three main benefits. The first one is comparable information. GAAP maintains consistency.

As a result, users can compare financial statements overtime for the same company, or with other companies for the same period. The second benefit is reliable information. GAAP reduces the chances of risk and fraud. Also, presented information is unbiased and objective. Unbiased means, a company can't select information to favor one user over another user. Objective means transactions are recorded based on solid evidence. Accountants can't record or present any information based on their personal opinion. As a result, users can trust the reported information in the financial statements.

Third benefit is providing relevant information, by disclosing all related information which makes a difference in the way users assess the company. This reported information affects the user's decision. These are three main benefits of adopting GAAP while preparing financial statements. Other than GAAP, there are other sets of standards established by the International Accounting Standards Board (IASB). These standards are called International Financial Reporting Standards (IFRS). As markets become more global, many countries outside the United States have adopted IFRS to be able to compare their financial statements with other countries.

This subject becomes more crucial for multinational companies located in the United States which have multiple branches around the world. The main branch in the U.S. has to follow GAAP, while other branches may follow IFRS or any other national standards. The setting bodies for these two standards have made huge efforts to reduce differences between U.S. GAAP and IFRS. This is the end of our chapter, thanks for reading and see you with the next one.

Basic Concepts of Accounting Part 1

We learned in our previous chapter what GAAP is. We will talk in this chapter about basic concepts of accounting. I will explain 12 main concepts, which will be splitted into 3 parts. Each part will contain 4 concepts. This is part one, let us get started. Our first concept is Economic Entity Assumption. It means a company keeps its activities separated from owners' personal activities. As a result, only business-related transactions are recorded, while owner's personal transactions outside the company are not recorded.

Let us assume a company purchased a land it will be registered by the company name rather than owner name, and this transaction will be recorded in the company books. In contrast, if the owner buys another land which is registered by his own name, it will not be recorded in the company books as per economic entity assumption. We also have another type of transactions between the company and its owner. These transactions are considered business related transactions. One example, the owner invested capital in a company.

Another example, when the owner withdraws cash from the company bank account. These types of transactions are recorded in the books of the company. Let us move to the second concept, which is Monetary Unit Assumption. Money provides an appropriate basis for measurements and analysis. This assumption requires companies to include only transaction data that can be expressed in money terms such as the U.S Dollar or any other currency. Some relevant information such as quality of service, or morals of employees are difficult to be quantified.

As a result, it can't be expressed in money value and can't be recorded. Furthermore, accounting ignores price level changes for inflation or deflation. It assumes the monetary unit such as the U.S Dollar and other currencies are reasonably stable. Our third concept is Going Concern Assumption. It assumes companies to last long enough to fulfill their objectives and commitments, which means companies will have a very long life. This assumption is used based on historical cost principle. When we assume liquidation of a business, the fair value principle is applied.

Liquidation approaches require companies to evaluate assets at fair value rather than acquisition cost. Fair value is the price to be received to sell an asset or paid to settle a liability on maturity date. Fair value is a market-based measurement. The going concern assumption applies on most business situations, only where liquidation approach is inapplicable. Let us see our fourth concept, which is Periodicity Assumption. If we want to measure the exact result of a company's activities, we have to wait until liquidation. To support decision makers, we can't wait such a long time. Users need to know the company performance on a timely basis to evaluate the business and to compare results.

Periodicity Assumption allows companies to report its economic activities using multiple time periods, such as monthly, quarterly, and yearly periods. The shorter a period, the more difficult it is to measure net income accurately for the same period. Furthermore, the quicker to report results, the more likely information to include errors and it would be less reliable. This is the end of our chapter, thanks for reading and see you with the next one.

Basic Concepts of Accounting Part 2

We learned in our previous chapter four basic concepts of accounting. In this chapter, we will learn additional four concepts which are accrual basis, historical cost, conservatism, and matching principle. Let us start with Accrual Basis of Accounting. It means transactions are recorded in the period in which events occur. Expenses are recorded when they are incurred rather than paid.

While revenues are recorded when they are earned rather than received in cash. Example of expense is payroll for the month of Dec 2019, it is recorded in Dec 2019 even though it will be paid in Jan 2020. Another example is sales of inventory in Dec 2019, its revenue is recorded in Dec 2019 even though it is collected in Jan 2020. There is an alternative approach, which is cash basis. Under cash basis expenses are recognized once cash is paid, while revenues are recognized once cash is collected.

If all business transactions are cash, both accrual and cash basis will have the same results. Cash basis is not allowed in both GAAP and IFRS. Our next concept is the Historical Cost Principle. It means assets and liabilities are reported on the basis of acquisition price. If we buy inventory in Jan 2019 for $100, it will be recorded by $100. After one year, the recorded value will be $100 as well. What if market value increased for these goods to become $150?

According to historical cost principle, goods value will not be adjusted for price increase. But what if market value for the same goods decreased to become $50? Company will follow a conservatism approach. In the inventory case, it will follow the rule of Lower Cost or Market, we call it (LCM). We will talk about Lower Cost or Market later in this Book. Our next concept is Conservatism. Accountants will recognize losses once anticipated rather than incurred. In contrast, potential gains are not allowed to be recognized until they are earned. One example is when the value of inventory is expected to be reduced, companies will follow a conservatism approach by using Lower of Cost or Market.

Another example, when inventory prices are increased no gains will be recognized until these goods are sold with higher prices. The final concept in this part is Expense Recognition. We can call it the Matching Principle as well. What is the expense? Expenses are assets consumed or liabilities incurred, or both as a result of selling goods, or rendering services. This concept is about expenses to follow revenues. Matching means linking efforts, which is expenses with accomplishments, which is revenues. One example is salaries for Dec 2019. It is linked with the sales of services rendered for the same period.

Even though salaries are paid on Jan 2020 and sales of services are collected also on Jan 2020, these expenses will be recorded in the same period in which revenues are earned which is Dec 2019 rather than at the time of collection. There are some cases it is difficult to match cost with its related revenue. Such as administration cost. In this case, such transactions are expensed as incurred. This is the end of our chapter, thanks for reading and see you with the next one.

Basic Concepts of Accounting Part 3

We learned eight basic concepts of accounting. Today we will learn additional four concepts, which are Revenue Recognition, Full Disclosure Principle, Materiality Principle, and finally Objectivity Principle. Our ninth concept is Revenue Recognition. Revenue recognition is a combination of accrual accounting and matching principle. Revenues are recognized in the period in which they are realized or realizable and earned, not in the period when cash is collected.

Revenues are realized when cash payment is received. Realizable means a collection of revenues is reasonably assured, especially when the company enters into a contract with a customer to sell goods or services with a specific amount of cash. Earned means goods are delivered, and services are rendered. Once these two rules are met together, the company will recognize revenue in the books. But what If cash is received in advance before the sale? it will be recorded as liability. This liability will be offsetted once revenue is earned.

Before moving to the next concept, I would like to mention that both FASB and IASB have jointly issued a framework for recognizing revenue from contracts with customers. It improves the comparability of financial statements across all industries with the effective year of 2018. Under GAAP the standard is ASC 606, while under international standards it is IFRS 15. This framework is a five-steps model that recognizes revenues in the period in which performance obligation is satisfied, as follows: the first step to identify the contract with the customer. The second step to identify the separate performance obligation in the contract. Third step to determine the transaction price. Fourth step is allocating transaction price to the separate performance obligation.

The final step is recognizing revenue once performance obligation is satisfied. This is just a brief idea about this framework. But for this Book we will focus on the main concept of recognizing revenues. Our next concept is Full Disclosure Principle. To decide which information to report, companies follow general practice of providing information which influences user's decisions. Users find financial information in three places, in the body of financial statements, or in the notes to these statements, or in the supplementary information. There are four financial statements in accounting.

We have a statement of financial position, which we call a balance sheet. There is also an income statement, statement of changes in equity, and finally a statement of cash flow. The notes to financial statements generally explain the presented information in the main body. These notes will be presented on a quantity or quality basis, such as description of accounting policies and procedures used to prepare the financial statements. Another example is explanation of uncertainties and contingencies included in the financial statements.

Supplementary information is any information presented in addition to the financial statements which is not considered necessary to fairly present the financial statements. It could be presented with the financial statements itself or in a separate document. A common example is an expanded schedule or table with full details for any line item in the financial statements. Such as a full breakdown of cost of goods sold or operating expenses in the income statement. The next concept is Materiality Principle. Materiality is a company-specific principle.

Information considered to be material if removing such data will impact users' decisions on financial statements. In contrast, information which has no influence on a user's decision will be considered immaterial. Assessing materiality is a challenging aspect in Accounting, it requires evaluating relative size and importance. To explain this subject let us see the following table. We have two companies A and B. Company A has a gross profit of one million dollars, while company B has a gross profit of $20,000. We notice there is unusual gain included in the sales figure for the value of $10,000 in both companies. We can consider it immaterial for company A since it is only 1% of gross profit. For company B it is a different scenario.

While unusual gain is the same for both companies, it is considered material in company B since it is 50% of gross profit. including such unusual gain in sales figure for B company will mislead the users of its financial statements. Normally companies and auditors have adopted a 5% cap of net income, any total amount below this percentage is considered immaterial. This threshold should not be used to hide important information from the users, such as hiding illegal transactions. Our last concept is the Objectivity Principle. It means information is reported in financial statements based on solid evidence rather than personal opinion of accountants or the management.

Their opinions could be optimistic or pessimistic rather than independent and unbiased. One example when the management is too optimistic and believes a massive gain could be earned from a lawsuit it may record the revenue accordingly even though the evidence doesn't assure such an outcome. Objectivity principles require the company to wait until solid evidence can be obtained to prove such gain. This is the end of our chapter, thanks for reading and see you with the next one.

Business Legal Forms

In the previous chapter, we learned about 12 basic concepts of accounting. In this chapter, we will talk about legal forms the business can take, and how it affects owners' liabilities and tax returns. When we explained economic entity assumption, we addressed that Accounting requires business related transactions to be separated from owners' personal transactions. There are several legal forms, we will discuss in this chapter four common forms.

Our first legal form is Proprietorship. It is a business owned by one person, which has a separate economic entity for Accounting purpose only. In contrast, it is not a separate legal entity from its owner. It has unlimited liabilities, which means the owner is personally liable for all debts of the business. Owners personal assets such as cars, buildings, cash in banks, are all at risk to cover business liabilities. A proprietorship income is not subject to business income tax, instead it is reported and taxed in the owner's personal tax return.

The second legal form is Partnership. It is a business owned by two or more persons. Like proprietorship, partnership has separate economic entities which require business related transactions to be separated from owners' personal transactions. In contrast, partnership is not legally separated from its owners. Each partner has unlimited personal liabilities for the debts of partnership. In contrast, each partner share of profit is reported and taxed in the partner's tax return. It is not subject to business income tax. Our third legal form is Corporation.

It has a separate economic entity, and It is legally separated from its owners. The owners of corporations are called shareholders, who are not personally liable to business debts. In corporations, board of directors are elected to oversee the company, and corporate officers are selected to run day to day operations. Ownership of a corporation is divided into transferable shares of stock. Stockholders may transfer all or part of their ownership at any time. Corporations suffer from the double taxation effect. There is a business income tax, and another tax on any distribution of income to shareholders through dividends.

Corporations are more suitable for companies, which require large amounts of capital or for companies who want to go public in the stock market. The last legal form is Limited Liabilities Company L.L.C. It is a hybrid business form between a corporation and proprietorship or partnership. It takes the advantages of these forms and leaves the disadvantages. It offers a limited liability of corporation, and tax treatments of proprietorship or partnership. L.L.C has protected liability to its owners. They are not personally liable to all business debts, and It avoids double taxation issues in corporations. Business income tax is reported and taxed in the owner's personal tax return.

One more point to add that proprietorship and partnership can be established as L.L.C. But, corporations can't be limited liability companies. To recap, let us see the following table.

We notice that all business forms have economic entities for Accounting purposes. For legal entities, it is available only for corporations and limited liability companies. There is no legal entity for proprietorship or partnership. Regarding limited liabilities, it is available for both corporations and L.L.C. For business tax, it is only available for corporations. Finally, for personal tax it is available in all business forms. This is the end of chapter 7, thanks for reading and see you with the next one.

Accounting Equation

In the previous chapter, we learned about business legal forms. In this chapter, we will talk about Accounting equations. Let us have a look at the following formula, assets equal liabilities plus owner's equity. Assets are resources owned by a business, while liabilities and owner's equity are claims against these resources. We can look at Accounting Equations in different directions. It can show the values of how assets were financed by liabilities and owner's equity. In Accounting Equation, liabilities usually appear before owner's equity because they are paid first before the claims of owners if the business is liquidated.

Regarding Assets, they are resources owned by a business and expected to generate future economic benefits. Such as cash, inventory, machines, equipment, and lands. Future economic benefits eventually result in future cash inflows. One example is inventory, it is purchased for the purpose of reselling to customers, which will result in cash collection. Another example is machines, it is used to produce products, which will be sold to generate cash in the business. Regarding Liabilities, it is creditors' claims against assets. It can be expressed as assets financed by creditors.

It represents future outflows of resources. Such as wages payable to employees, accounts payable to suppliers, loans payable to banks, and tax payable to government. Regarding Owner's Equity, it represents owners claims against assets. It can be expressed as assets financed by owners. If we change the accounting equation to represent Owner's Equity, it will equal Assets minus Liabilities. For this reason, owner's equity is called Net Assets or Residual Equity. It is the remaining assets after subtracting all liabilities.

In Proprietorship, owner investments and revenues increase equity, while owner withdrawals and expenses decrease equity. Investment by owners are assets the owner adds to the business. It is normally recorded in an accounting ledger called Owner's Capital. For Revenues, it is the gross increase in equity resulting from a business earning activities. Revenues result in increase of assets, or reduction of liabilities, or both. For example, revenue from rendering of programing services. It will generate cash inflows and it will increase assets accordingly. Or when the company receives cash in advance from customers and records it as liability, this liability will be reduced and settled once revenue is rendered.

Regarding Owner Drawings, it is assets withdrawn by the owner for personal use. Such as cash drawn from a company bank account to be used personally by the owner. Regarding Expenses, it is the cost of assets consumed, or services used for the purpose of earning revenues. Such as salaries of employees, uses of supplies and goods, cost of utilities, advertisement, rent, and bank interest. Expenses usually result in reduction of assets, or increase of liabilities, or both. For example, advertisement expenses will result in cash payment, and assets will decrease accordingly. Or, if this advertisement was purchased on credit, accounts payable will increase and liabilities will increase accordingly.

At the end, we can expand Owner's Equity in Accounting Equation to be as follows, assets equal liabilities plus owner's capital plus revenues minus owner's drawings minus expenses. This is the end of chapter eight, thanks for reading and see you next time.

Transaction Analysis Using Accounting Equation

In the previous chapter we learned about Accounting Equations. In this chapter, we will talk about transaction analysis using accounting equations. At the beginning, let us remember what the accounting equation is. It is assets equal to liabilities plus owner's equity. We can see the expanded version of the accounting equation as follows, assets equal liabilities plus owner's capital plus revenues minus owner's drawings minus expenses.

In this chapter we will analyze multiple transactions and see how it affects the accounting equation. Our first transaction is an investment by the owner. The owner decided to open a company to provide advertising services. On 1st Dec 2018, he invested $10,000 cash in the business. This transaction results in an equal increase in assets and owner's equity. Cash will increase by $10,000 and the owner's capital will increase by $10,000. If we apply this analysis on the accounting equation and under the assets group, we see how cash increased by $10,000.

For liabilities, there is no effect because the investment was done by the owner not by creditors. Under owner's equity, this investment will increase owner's capital by $10,000. You can observe the equality of accounting equations has been maintained. $10,000 on the left side, and $10,000 on the right side. The second transaction is purchase of equipment for cash. On 2nd Dec 2018, the company purchased printing equipment for $4,000 cash. This transaction results in equal increase & decrease in total assets. Cash will decrease by $4,000, and equipment will increase by $4,000.

If we apply this analysis on the accounting equation, we will notice how the cash balance is reduced from $10,000 to become $6,000. Equipment balance became $4,000 after this transaction. This transaction has no effect on liabilities or owner's equity. Observe the equality of accounting equations. The value of total assets is $10,000 while total value of liabilities and owner's equity is $10,000 as well. The next transaction is purchase of office supplies on credit. On 3rd Dec 2018, the company purchased office supplies for $2,000 on credit. It is expected to last several months.

The vendor is allowed to pay this bill in future. This transaction will increase assets because these supplies are expected to have future economic benefits. as indicated, it will last several months after the date of purchasing. Additionally, this transaction will increase liabilities because the purchase was on credit. As a result, office supplies will increase by $2,000 and accounts payable will increase by $2,000. If we apply this analysis on the accounting equation, we will notice under the assets group how office supplies increased by $2,000.

Under liabilities, accounts payable balance become $2,000 after this transaction. Observe the equality of accounting equations. The value of total assets is $12,000, while total value of liabilities and owner's equity is $12,000 as well. Our next transaction is providing advertising services for cash. On 15th Dec 2018, the company provided advertisement services to one customer for $1,000 cash. This transaction will increase revenues by $1,000 because advertisement services represent earning activities of the company. revenues will increase owner's equity accordingly. Additionally, cash will increase because the company received cash against these services. If we apply this transaction to the accounting equation, we will notice under the assets group how the cash balance increased by $1,000.

Under owner's equity, revenues balance become $1,000 after this transaction. Observe the equality of accounting equations. The value of total assets is $13,000 while total value of liabilities and owner's equity is $13,000 as well. The next transaction is providing advertising services on credit. On 16th Dec 2018, the company provided advertisement services to another customer for $2,000 on credit. This transaction will increase revenues by $2,000 because advertisement services represent earning activities of the company. revenues will increase owner's equity accordingly.

Additionally, accounts receivable will increase because the company allowed its customer to pay the bill in future. If we apply this transaction on the accounting equation, we will notice under the assets group how accounts receivable increased by $2,000 Under owner's equity, the revenues balance increased from $1,000 to become $3,000. Observe the equality of accounting equations. The value of total assets is $15,000 while total value of liabilities and owner's equity is $15,000 as well. Our next transaction is payment to the vendor. On 19th Dec 2018, the company paid its vendor $500 by cash. which is a partial settlement of their bill. This transaction will reduce both cash and accounts payable by $500. If we apply this transaction on an accounting equation, we notice under the assets group how the cash balance will be reduced from $7,000 to become $6,500.

Under liabilities, accounts payable balance will be reduced from $2,000 to become $1,500. Observe the equality of accounting equations. The value of total assets is $14,500 while total value of liabilities and owner's equity is $14,500 as well. The next transaction is receipt of cash from the customer. On 20th Dec 2018, the company received $1,500 cash from its customer against previous services performed on 16th Dec 2018. This transaction will increase cash by $1,500 and reduce accounts receivable by $1,500. If we apply this transaction on an accounting equation, we will notice under the assets group how the cash balance increased from $6,500 to become $8,000.

Additionally, accounts receivable balance decreased from $2,000 to become $500. Observe the equality of accounting equations. The value of total assets is $14,500 while total value of liabilities and owner's equity is $14,500 as well. Our next transaction is cash withdrawal by the owner. On 25th Dec 2018, the owner withdrew $1,000 cash from the company for personal use. This transaction will reduce cash by $1,000 and increase owner's drawings by $1,000. The owner's drawings will reduce the owner's equity accordingly. If we apply this transaction on an accounting equation, we will notice under the assets group how the cash balance decreased from $8,000 to become $7,000.

Under owner's equity, the owner's withdrawal balance becomes $1,000 after this transaction. Observe the equality of accounting equations. The value of total assets is $13,500 while total value of liabilities and owner's equity is $13,500 as well. Our final transaction is payment of salaries expenses. On 31st Dec 2018, the company paid salaries to its employees for $2,500 by cash. This transaction will increase expenses by $2,500 because salaries are utilized to perform earning activities in the company. It represents the cost of providing advertising services.

Owner's equity will be reduced accordingly. Additionally, cash will be reduced by the same amount $2,500. If we apply this transaction on an accounting equation, we will notice under the assets group how the cash balance reduced from $7,000 to become $4,500 Under owner's equity, salaries expenses balance become $2,500 after this transaction.

Observe the equality of accounting equations. The value of total assets is $11,000 while total value of liabilities and owner's equity is $11,000 as well. This is the end of chapter nine, thanks for reading and see you with the next one.

Debits and Credits

In the previous chapter we learned transaction analysis using accounting equations. In this chapter we will talk about debits and credits. To understand debits and credits, we have to learn first what is the meaning of Account? It is an individual accounting record, which is used to sort and store transactions of specific asset, liability, or owner's equity items. The simple form account consists of three parts: title of the account, the left side which is called "debit side", and the right side which is called "credit side".

Because the shape of the account represents the letter T, we call it T-account. This form is useful for illustration purposes. However, there is another standard form which is called a three column ledger account. We will see this form later in this Book once we talk about posting to ledgers. The term debit means left, and the term credit means right. Debits and credits don't mean increase or decrease, but they describe where the transaction is booked on the left side or on the right side of the account. For example, the act of entering an amount on the left side is called debiting the account while recording an entry on the right side is called crediting the account.

Debits and credits are commonly abbreviated as Dr. for debit and Cr. for credit. These abbreviations come from old recordkeeping practice, where the terms "debtor" and "creditor" were used instead of debit and credit. The abbreviations use the first and last letters of these terms. By comparing the total amounts of the two sides, the account shows a debit balance if the total of debit amounts exceeds the total of credit amounts. The position of debit balance is shown on the left side, which is the "debit side". In contrast, the account shows a credit balance if the total of credit amounts exceeds the total of debit amounts.

The position of credit balance is shown on the right side, which is the "credit side". To illustrate account balance, let us see the following example of a cash account. The transaction data is taken from our previous chapter. In the tabular summary, each positive transaction represents a receipt of cash and each negative amount represents a payment of cash. Notice that in T-account, we record the increases of cash as debits and the decreases of cash as credits. The first value is $10,000 representing a cash receipt, and it is recorded on the debit side of the account. The next value is $4,000 representing a cash payment, and it is recorded on the credit side of the account.

The next value is $1,000 representing a cash receipt, and it is recorded on the debit side of the account. The next value is $500 representing a cash payment, and it is recorded on the credit side of the account. The next value is $1,500 representing a cash receipt, and it is recorded on the debit side of the account. The next two values are $1,000 and $2,500 represent cash payments, which are recorded on the credit side of the account. The balance of a cash account is the difference value between total debits and total credits. In our case it is a $4,500 debit balance, and it is shown on the debit side. To understand on which side the account increases and decreases, we have to learn what is the normal balance of the account?

Let us first remember the accounting equation. It is assets equal liabilities plus owner's equity. All accounts related to the left side of the equation will increase on the left side, which is called the "debit side" and these accounts normally show debit balances. All accounts related to the right side of the equation will increase on the right side, which is called the "credit side" and these accounts normally show credit balances. Normal balance of an account is on the side where increases are recorded. Regarding assets accounts, they increase on the debit side and decrease on the credit side.

Assets accounts normally show debit balances. Regarding liabilities accounts, they increase on the credit side and decrease on the debit side. Liabilities accounts normally show credit balances. Regarding owner's equity, let us remember that investment by owner and revenues increase owner's equity, while owner's drawings and expenses reduce owner's equity. As a result, both owner's capital and revenues accounts increase on the credit side and decrease on the debit side. They normally show credit balances accordingly.

In contrast, Owner's drawings and expenses accounts increase on the debit side and decrease on the credit side. They normally show debit balances accordingly. To summarize debit and credit rules and effects for each type of account, let us see the following: we will start with the basic accounting equation, and then expand the equation to indicate all owner's equity accounts. We can see the effect on assets, owner's drawings, and expenses accounts, they increase on the debit side and decrease on the credit side. These accounts normally show debit balances.

In contrast, liabilities, owner's capital, and revenues accounts increase on the credit side and decrease on the debit side. These accounts normally show credit balances. One last point to add: When we discussed transaction analysis using accounting equations in our previous chapter, remember that each transaction must affect two or more accounts to keep the accounting equation in balance. In other words, debits must equal credits for each transaction. The equality of debits and credits provide the basis for "double-entry system". Under the double-entry system, each transaction is recorded in appropriate accounts with dual effect by debiting one account and crediting another account.

As a result, the sum of all debits to the accounts must equal the sum of all the credits. This system helps to insure accuracy and reduce errors while recording transactions. This is the end of chapter ten, thanks for reading and see you with the next one.

Introduction to Financial Statements

In the previous chapter, we learned debits and credits. In this chapter, we will take an introduction to financial statements. There are four financial statements, which are used by both internal and external users. Our first statement is an income statement, it reports revenues, expenses, and resulting net income or net loss for a specific period of time. We also have a statement of changes in equity, which reports changes of the owner's capital account for a specific period of time.

Our next statement is the balance sheet, it is also called the statement of financial position. It reports assets, liabilities, and owner's equity at a specific date. Our last report is a statement of cash flows, which reports cash receipts and cash payments from operating, investing, and financing activities for a specific period of time To illustrate these four statements, we will use our sample data from previous chapters. Remember our accounting equation example, under assets group cash balance is $4,500.

Printing equipment balance is $4,000. Office supplies balance is $2,000, and accounts receivable balance is $500. Total assets balance is $11,000. Regarding liabilities, accounts payable balance is $1,500. For the owner's equity group, the owner's capital balance is $10,000. Owner's drawing balance is $1,000. Advertisement revenues balance is $3,000 and salaries expenses balance is $2,500. Total liabilities and owner's equity balance is $11,000.

We will start with an income statement. Revenues are reported first, in our example they include $3,000 advertisement revenues. Expenses are reported after revenues, in our example they include $2,500 salaries expenses. Net income or net loss is reported at the bottom of the statement. In our example it is $500 net income. Our next report is a statement of changes in equity. It starts with the beginning balance of the owner's capital account. Then, it is increased by the owner's investment and net income. In contrast, it is decreased by the owner's drawings and net loss. In our example, the beginning balance of the owner's capital account is zero.

It will increase by investment by the owner which is $10,000 and increase by net income which is $500. Observe the connection between income statement and statement of changes in equity, where net income balance is presented accordingly. The total increase is $10,500. Furthermore, the owner's drawings of $1,000 will be deducted, and the ending balance of the owner's capital account will become $9,500. Observe the connection between the statement of changes in equity and the balance sheet, where the ending balance of the owner's capital account will be transferred to the balance sheet, and it will be presented under the equity group.

Additionally, notice that the equity structure in this example is used by proprietorship and partnership. For corporations, we are using different equity structures and different accounts, such as share capital, share premium, dividends, and retained earning accounts. We will present in this Book the simple equity structure of proprietorship. Our next statement is the balance sheet. It starts with assets at the top, then followed by liabilities and owner's equity. In our example there are four assets accounts. Cash balance with $4,500.

Accounts receivable balance with $500. Office supplies balance with $2,000 and printing equipment balance with $4,000. For liabilities, we have accounts payable balance with $1,500. For owner's equity, the ending balance of owner's capital $9,500 is taken from the statement of changes in equity. Notice that, total assets equal to total liabilities and owner's equity with the value of $11,000. This is exactly matching with our accounting equation example. Observe the connection between the balance sheet and statement of cash flows, where cash ending balance is matching in both statements.

Our last report is a statement of cash flows. It starts with cash flows from operating activities. Then followed by cash flows from investing activities, Then followed by cash flows from financing activities. The sum of these three values will result in a net increase or decrease of cash. Then, we will add a cash opening balance to reach the bottom-line cash ending balance, which must match the same value of the cash account in the balance sheet. In our example, under cash flows from operating activities we have three values. Our first value is cash receipts from customers with a value of $2,500.

Notice that this figure comes from the same nine transaction data, which is taken from our previous chapters. Our next value is $500 cash paid to vendors. Then we have $2,500 cash paid to employees as salaries. The net cash generated by operating activities is negative $500 . Our next group is cash flows from investing activities, which include $4,000 purchase of printing equipment by cash. The next group is cash flows from financing activities, which include $10,000 investment by the owner and $1,000 drawings by the owner. The net cash generated by financing activities is $9,000. Then, we will calculate the net increase in cash from all activities, which is $4,500.

We will add to this figure the cash beginning balance on December 1st, which is zero in our example, to reach the bottom-line cash ending balance as of December 31st. This statement includes a lot of complications, but for now I would like you to understand the basic form of this statement and how it is linked with other statements. At the end, notice how these four statements are interrelated. Net income of $500 on the income statement is added to the beginning balance of the owner's capital in the statement of changes in equity.

The next connection is the owner's capital balance of $9,500 in the statement of changes in equity reported on the balance sheet under the equity group. The last relationship is cash balance of $4,500 in the balance sheet is reported as cash ending balance on the statement of cash flows. This is the end of our chapter, thanks for reading and see you with the next one.

Chart of Accounts

In this chapter, we will learn the chart of accounts. It is a master list of all accounts a company uses to record its transactions in the accounting system. This list includes account code and account name. In most countries, the number and type of accounts differ from one company to another. It is up to the accountants and management to decide the level of details required to report.

A small business might use 20 to 30 accounts to report its transactions. A larger business may require thousands of accounts. The numbering system usually starts with the balance sheet accounts and followed by income statement accounts. For example, the following numbering system uses a three digits code. In this case the first digit is used for account type, such as number one for assets, number two for liabilities, number three for owner's equity, number four for revenues, and number five for expenses.

The next two digits are used for subcategories. Let us see the following example of three digits code, the range from 100 to 199 assigned to asset accounts, the range from 200 to 299 assigned to liability accounts, the range from 300 to 399 assigned to equity accounts, the range from 400 to 499 assigned to revenue accounts, the range from 500 to 599 assigned to expense accounts. The following list shows an example of a chart of accounts.

- Account code 101 indicate cash,

- account code 115 indicate accounts receivable,
- 120 indicate inventory,
- 150 indicate equipment,
- 201 indicate accounts payable,
- 205 indicate notes payable,
- 301 indicate owner's capital account,
- 305 indicate owner's drawings account,
- 401 indicate service revenue,
- 501 indicate salaries expense,
- 511 indicate rent expense,
- 525 indicate utilities expense,
- 590 indicates interest expense.

Notice that there are gaps in the chart of accounts. Companies normally leave gaps to be able to insert new accounts as needed in the future. This is the end of our chapter, thanks for reading and see you with the next one.

What is the Accounting Cycle?

In this chapter we will study the recording process in the accounting system. To record transactions and to prepare financial statements, companies follow multiple procedures, as follow: the first step is selecting and analyzing transactions the next step is journalizing transactions the next step is posting journal entries to ledger accounts after that we will prepare trial balance before adjustments the next step to record adjusting entries for accruals and deferrals then we prepare trial balance after adjustments next we prepare financial statements then we pass closing entries to close the period after that we can prepare post-closing trial balance which is an optional process finally we can use reversing entries in the accounting cycle, which is also an optional process.

Notice that once these steps have been completed the sequence starts over again in the next accounting period. The first process of analyzing transactions is already discussed in our previous chapter. We will learn the other steps in detail in this chapter. This is the end of our chapter, thanks for reading and see you with the next one.

Journalizing

Afterwards, we discussed the accounting cycle. We will learn the journalizing process in this chapter. Journalizing is the process of recording transactions in chronological order. Chronological means the order in which transactions occur. Each transaction is recorded in a separate journal entry. Using the journal to record business transactions is useful for multiple reasons: it discloses the effect of all transactions in one place, it provides a chronological record, and it helps to reduce errors by using debit and credit rules.

Companies may use different kinds of journals but all of them use the basic form which is called a general journal. In some cases, a company may use special journals in addition to general journals. Such as cash receipt journal, cash payment journal, sales journal, and purchases journal. We will focus in our Book on general journals, let us see what it consists of? First, it includes the date of transaction. It also includes the account title and explanation. Then we have a reference number which is used for account code. then we have the debit amount, and the credit amount.

Finally, it includes the journal page number. To understand how to journalize transactions, let us see the following example. An owner decided to open a company to provide programming services. On 1st Jan 2019, he invested $15,000 cash in the business. Let us first analyze which accounts get affected by this transaction. Cash account will increase by $15,000 since the owner invested cash. and then the owner's capital account will increase by $15,000 as well since the owner 's investment will affect the capital account.

After analyzing the transaction, we can start entering this transaction into the journal. At the beginning, we will enter the date in the first column which is January first. Then, we enter the debit account title and its value which is in our case the cash account with a value of $15,000. Why is cash debited? Because cash is an assets account which increases on the debit side. Notice that the dollar sign is not used in the journal entry. The next step is to enter the credit account title and its value. which is in our case the owner's capital account with a value of $15,000. Why is the owner's capital credited? Because the owner's capital is an equity account, which increases on the credit side.

Notice that the title of the credit account is indented from the left margin. This practice is useful to differentiate credit accounts from debit accounts. Notice also debit accounts are always presented before credit accounts. After recording the credit value, we enter a brief explanation. In our case, we can write the owner 's investment by cash. The final step to keep the reference number blank. Normally accountants will fill reference numbers at the time of posting. Remember that reference number is used for account code. Account title and account code come from the chart of accounts. At the end, notice how the double-entry system is maintained. The debit value must equal the credit value which is in our case $15,000. This journal entry is considered a simple entry because it affects two accounts only.

In other cases, the transaction may affect three or more accounts. In such cases the entry is called compound entry. To explain compound entries, let us see the following example. On 5th Jan 2019, the company purchased equipment with a total value of $3,000. It paid $2,000 by cash and the remaining value $1,000 on account to be paid later. In this case, there are three accounts that get affected. The first account is equipment, which increased by $3,000. The second account is cash, which decreased by $2,000. and the third account is accounts payable, which increased by $1,000 since the remaining value was on account.

In our journal, we enter the date first, which is January fifth. Then we enter the debit account, which is equipment with a value of $3,000. We debited equipment because it is an asset account which increases on the debit side. Next, we enter both credit accounts. The first one is cash with a value of $2,000. We credited cash because it is an asset account which decreases on the credit side. The second credit account is accounts payable with a value of $1,000. We credited accounts payable because it is a liability account, which increases on the credit side.

The explanation of our transaction is purchase of equipment by cash with a balance on account. The reference number is kept blank until we post this transaction. At the end, notice that total debit amounts must equal total credit amounts. This is the end of our chapter, thanks for reading and see you with the next one. This is the end of our chapter, thanks for reading and see you with the next one.

Posting to General Ledger

After we learn what journaling is in the accounting cycle, we will discuss posting to the general ledger. Posting is the process of transferring journal entries to the ledger accounts. We studied before the simple form of a ledger account, which is called the T-account. We will see in this chapter the standard form, which is called a three-column ledger account. It is called that because it has three money value columns, debit, credit, and balance. The balance amount is calculated after each transaction. This form includes the following, the date, explanation, reference number which is used to indicate journal page number where the source data was transferred. Then we have the debit value, credit value, balance value, and finally the account code number.

Now let us see the steps of posting transactions. We will use our simple entry example from the previous chapter. Notice that the debited account was cash, and the credited account was the owner's capital account. At the beginning, we start with a cash general ledger account. We enter all the data from the journal entry, which is the date 1st Jan 2019, then we enter the journal page number J1 in the reference column. After that, we enter the debit value of $15,000 since the cash account was debited in the journal entry.

The credit column is kept blank because there is no credit effect on the cash account. At the end of this step, the balance value is calculated after each transaction. In our case, it is $15,000. Notice that the explanation column is used infrequently because it is already available in journal entries. Notice also, the dollar sign is not used in the general ledger. The second step in the journal entry is to record the account code number in the reference column, which is related to the debit account.

In our case, it is 101 for a cash general ledger account. Our third step involves the general ledger of the owner's capital account. We enter all the data from the journal entry, which is the date 1st Jan 2019, then we enter journal page number J1 in the reference column. After that, we keep the debit value blank because there is no debit effect on the owner's capital account. Then we enter the credit value of $15,000 since the owner's capital account was credited in the journal entry.

At the end of this step, the balance value is calculated after each transaction. In our case, it is $15,000. The fourth step in the journal entry is to record the account code number in the reference column, which is related to the credit account. In our case, it is 301 for the owner's capital account. The last step in the posting process, we review and make sure all reference numbers are filled in the journal which means all transactions are posted. This process is useful to avoid errors before preparing the trial balance. If we want to apply the posting process on the T-account, we can follow the same procedures as follow.

The first step is to enter the date and debit value of $15,000 in the cash account, then we enter the account code in the journal entry reference column which is 101. After that, we enter the date and credit value of $15,000 in the owner’s capital account. Then, we enter the account code in the journal entry reference column which is 301. The last step, to verify all reference numbers are filled in the journal to make sure all transactions are posted. This is the end of our chapter, thanks for reading and see you next time.

Using Subsidiary Ledgers

We learned in our previous chapter posting to the general ledger. In this chapter, we will discuss using subsidiary ledgers. So, what do we mean by subsidiary ledger? It is a group of accounts with a common characteristic. We can indicate it as an expansion to a general ledger account. So, why are subsidiary ledgers used? Imagine we have hundreds, or even thousands of customers and we need to know the details of sales and collections for each customer.

Maintaining such large information in one general ledger account is considered impractical. On the other hand, creating a general ledger account for each customer is considered impractical as well. But why? Because our chart of accounts and trial balance will contain a large list of accounts, and it will be more difficult to prepare financial statements. The best practice is to keep one general ledger account to control multiple subsidiary accounts.

The sum of all subsidiary account's balances must equal the balance of one general ledger account. Let us see the following example. We have a general ledger account, which is accounts receivable with a balance of $6,000. This is a control account of three subsidiary accounts, which are customer A with a balance of $1,000 and customer B with a balance of $2,000 and customer C with a balance of $3,000. Notice that, the total balance of $6,000 for these three customers equals the balance of their general ledger account, which is accounts receivable.

Up to this point, we learned what a subsidiary ledger is and why we use it. But what about posting? If we choose to create subsidiary ledgers in our accounting system, there will be dual posting. First posting to the subsidiary ledgers, and another posting to general ledgers. To clarify this subject, let us see the following example. We have four general ledger accounts, cash account, accounts receivable, accounts payable, and owner's capital.

Cash account in this example has no subsidiary account, the posting is done directly to the cash general ledger account. For accounts receivable there are three subsidiary accounts, customer A, customer B, and customer C. In this case there is dual posting, one posting to subsidiary accounts and another posting to a general ledger account. For accounts payable it is the same case, dual posting is done to subsidiary accounts and to the general ledger account. Finally, for the owner's capital we are posting directly to the general ledger account.

Regarding accounts receivable and payable, usually we post to their subsidiary ledgers on a daily basis to keep customer and vendor accounts up to date, and we post their balances to general ledger accounts on a monthly basis. In most recent accounting software, dual posting is done in real time. Once we post to the subsidiary ledger, the general ledger will be updated automatically. We saw in this example subsidiary ledgers are used for accounts receivable and payable. Actually we are using subsidiary ledgers more often with other accounts as well, such as inventory, fixed assets, and even cash and bank accounts. To have a better idea about dual posting, let us see the following example. On 10th Jan 2019, the company sold customer A programing services on account for the amount of $5,000.

Notice that there are two accounts that get affected. Accounts receivable and sales revenue, which are both increased by the same value of $5,000. As a result, accounts receivable for customer A is debited by $5,000 since it is an asset account, and sales revenue is credited by the same value of $5,000 since it is an equity account. Now, the first step is to enter the date, explanation, journal page number, and the debit value of $5,000 in the subsidiary account for customer A and also the same value in the general ledger for accounts receivable, then we enter the account code 102 and a check mark in the journal entry reference column.

What do we mean by this reference? Accounts receivable code number indicate posting is done to the general ledger, while the check mark indicates the posting is done for the subsidiary account, which is in this case customer A. You can notice the code number for customer A is totally different than accounts receivable code. Normally we generate separate sequences for each group of subsidiary ledgers. In this example we are using five digits code for customer ledgers starting with digit number seven. For vendors, we can start with different numbers, for example digit number eight.

Our third step is to enter the date, explanation, journal page number, and the credit value of $5,000 in the sales revenue account. Then, we enter the account code in the journal entry reference column which is 401. The last step, to verify all reference numbers are filled in the journal to make sure all transactions are posted in both subsidiary accounts and general ledger accounts. We considered in this example that dual posting is done in real time. Let us see now what will happen if we post monthly to general ledger accounts. To explain this topic, we will have in this example an additional subsidiary account, which is customer B.

This customer has two transactions. A credit sale of $10,000 on 15th Jan 2019, and a cash collection of $7,000 on 26th Jan 2019. The balance for customer B is $3,000. Now at the month end 31st Jan 2019, we post the total value of all debit transactions to the general ledger account, which is $15,000. Then, we post the total value of all credit transactions to the general ledger account, which is $7,000. Notice that, the balance of the general ledger for accounts receivable is $8,000 which equals the balance of both subsidiary accounts for customer A and customer B. At the end, let us see the advantages of using subsidiary accounts.

First, it provides up to date details on specific accounts rather than recording all similar transactions in one general ledger account. Second, trial balance will contain less general ledger accounts which result in easier preparation of financial statements. Finally, it helps to locate errors by using control accounts and by splitting posting responsibilities to be done by two accountants. One accountant is posting daily to subsidiary ledgers, and another accountant will post monthly to general ledgers. This is the end of our chapter, thanks for reading and see you with the next one.

Trial Balance

After we learned journalizing and posting in previous chapters, we will discuss for this chapter the trial balance. It is a list of all general ledger accounts and their balances at a given time. Normally accounts with zero balances are not listed in the trial balance. Trial balance can be prepared at any given time or date, but companies usually prepare it at the end of the accounting period which will help to prepare financial statements.

General ledger accounts are listed in the same order in which they appear in the chart of accounts. Debit and credit balances are separated in the trial balance, debit balances appear on the left column and credit balances appear on the right column. Total debit balances must equal total credit balances, this equality in trial balance is mandatory under the double-entry system. Notice that the dollar sign is used in trial balance for the first figure in each column and also in the totals.

Trial balance is considered a useful checkpoint since its equality would help to catch recording errors. For example, the accountant posted only the debit portion of a journal entry without posting the credit portion. In this case, the trial balance can detect such errors. On the other hand, even though total debits equal total credits there are some types of mistakes that may still exist, such as a transaction is not journalized at all. As a result, there is no posting to the general ledger.

Another example is when a correct journal entry is not posted. In this case the trial balance is still matching. One more example is when a journal entry is posted twice to the general ledger. In this case also total debit & credit balances in trial balance are still matching. Our last example when the accountant used an incorrect account in journalizing or posting. In this case both debit and credit balances will match in trial balance. These are four types of mistakes that can exist even though the sum of debit balances equals the sum of credit balances. This is the end of our chapter, thanks for reading and see with the next one.

Accrual vs Cash Basis

Before learning to adjust entries, we have to understand the difference between accrual basis and cash basis. Accrual basis recognizes revenue once earned rather than received in cash. Expenses are recognized once incurred rather than paid. In contrast, a cash basis recognizes revenue once collected and expenses once paid by cash. Cash basis seems to be a simple approach, but it reports misleading financial statements. It fails to record revenues for a business which performs the services but does not collect cash against these services.

Cash basis is not allowed under GAAP or IFRS. On the other hand, accrual basis reflects real business performance by recording events in the same period in which they occur. It also increases the comparability of financial statements from one period to another. Since cash basis is still important for decision makers, companies must report the statement of cash flows. To understand the difference between accrual and cash basis let us see the following example. On 1st Dec 2018, a company paid $1,200 for one year office rent starting from Dec 2018 and ending Nov 2019.

We will see in this example how the company will recognize office rent expense under both accrual basis and cash basis. Under an accrual basis we will recognize rent expenses among twelve months which means $100 every month. Notice in these two tables we recognize $100 rent expense in 2018 while it is $1,100 for 2019. Let us see now how we recognize rent expenses under cash basis. In this case the full value $1,200 will be recognized in one month which is Dec 2018. For 2019 there is no rent expense to be recognized. Why do we book the whole expense in Dec 2018? Because the cash basis recognizes the expense once paid by cash. We see in this example how a cash basis can mislead the users of financial statements.

The cost was recognized in one month rather than distributing this cost among all related periods. As a result, net income in 2018 under cash basis will be lower than net income under accrual basis for the same period. For 2019, it is the opposite. Net income under cash basis will be higher than accrual basis. These are the main differences between accrual basis and cash basis. This is the end of our chapter, thanks for reading and see you with the next one.

Why Adjusting Entries

Before we talk about the structure of adjusting entries, we should understand why we need to record adjusting entries every time we prepare financial statements. Companies need to record revenues in the same period in which services are performed, and also to record expenses in the period in which they are incurred. So, we use adjusting entries to achieve these requirements.

What do we understand from this subject? There are three accounting principles that affect the recording process of adjusting entries. The first principle is periodicity assumption, which we call time period assumption. Under this assumption, the economic life of a business can be divided into multiple time periods such as one month, three months, or one year. Monthly and quarterly periods are called interim periods, while one-year periods are called fiscal years.

Fiscal year is a twelve month period which begins with the first day of a month and ends 12 months later. For most companies, their fiscal year matches the calendar year from 1st January until 31st December. Other companies may use different fiscal years. For example, from 1st July until 30 June. Another example is a fiscal year ending January 31st, but why? There are some companies with high seasonal variation in sales. It is better for them to choose a fiscal year end when sales activities are at the lowest level, especially after the holiday season. This 12 month fiscal year will show more constant results from one period to another.

The second principle is revenue recognition. Under this principle, revenues are recognized in the period in which services are performed and when materials are delivered. Or we can indicate it as once performance obligation is satisfied as per IFRS. Our third principle is expense recognition, we call it also matching principle. Under this principle, we match expenses with revenues in the same period when expenses make a contribution to generate revenues. To explain it in a simple way, we can say:- let the expenses follow the revenues. These are three principles which raise the need to record adjusting entries.

But what about the trial balance before adjustment? It may not contain up to date and complete data. But why? Let us see the following reasons. Some transactions are not journalized daily. For example, monthly salaries for employees. Another reason, some expenses are not journalized during the accounting period because these costs expire with the passage of time. Such as rent and insurance contracts. Our final reason, some items may be unrecorded. For example, a utility bill is not received until the next accounting period. This is the end of our chapter, thanks for reading and see you with the next one.

Structure of Adjusting Entries

After we learned why we need to record adjusting entries, we will talk today about the types of these adjustments. Adjusting entries are classified either as deferrals or accruals. To understand how to differentiate these two groups let us see the following. We notice on the left side if cash is paid or received before recognizing expenses or revenues, there will be prepaid expenses or unearned revenues.

We call them deferrals, but why? Because the recognition of expenses and revenues are postponed for future periods until expenses incurred and revenues earned. Now for the right side, if cash is paid or received after the related expenses or revenues are recognized, there will be accrued expenses or accrued revenues. We call them accruals because cash was not paid or received at the time of recognition of expenses or revenues.

We will see in our next chapters how to record deferrals and accruals with examples, and you will notice how each adjusting entry will affect one or more income statement accounts and one or more balance sheet accounts, but for sure not the cash account. This is the end of our chapter, thanks for reading and see you next time.

Deferrals - Prepaid Expenses

After we learn the structure of adjusting entries, we will discuss the details of both deferrals and accruals. For this chapter, we will study the first group of deferrals which is prepaid expenses. So, what do we mean by deferrals? Defer means to postpone or delay. Deferrals are expenses or revenues that are recognized at a date later than when cash was paid or collected.

When companies make payments of expenses which benefit more than one accounting period, they record an asset which is called prepaid expense. Such as insurance, rent, advertisement, and supplies. In addition, the purchase of building and equipment is considered a part of deferrals. But it is categorized under fixed assets. We will talk about fixed assets and depreciation in future chapters later in this Book. So prepaid expense is a cost which expires either with the passage of time such as rent and insurance, or by consumption such as supplies.

The expiration of these costs do not require daily entries, which would be impractical. Instead, companies postpone the recognition of these expenses until they prepare financial statements. Let us now see the effect of adjusting entries on prepaid expenses. Since assets are overstated and expenses are understated at the time of preparing financial statements, an adjusting entry for prepaid expenses results in an increase or debit to expenses account, and a decrease of credit to the asset account.

Let us have a look at specific types of prepaid expenses. We will start with insurance. Normally insurance premium is paid in advance. As a result, it is recorded as an asset at the time of payment. So what will happen at the date of preparing financial statements? We will record the adjusting entry by debiting insurance expenses and crediting prepaid insurance accounts. To understand this subject, let us see the following example. On 1st Feb 2019, the company paid insurance premium in advance for one year for the amount of $2,400.

At the time of payment, the company records this advance payment as an asset, which we call it prepaid insurance as follows: we see in this example how prepaid insurance increased by $2,400 and cash account decreased by the same amount $2,400. In the journal entry, we debit prepaid insurance by $2,400 and credit cash account by $2,400. We can write an explanation "insurance premium for one year". Now at the date of preparing financial statements on 28th Feb 2019, there is one month passed out of twelve which means we have to recognize insurance expenses for the amount of $200 which result from dividing $2,400 over twelve months.

We see in this case, there are two accounts that get affected, insurance expenses will increase by $200, and prepaid insurance will decrease by $200. We can write an explanation "insurance expense for Feb 2019". As a result of this entry, the balance of prepaid insurance will be $2,200 which represents the value of the remaining period of eleven months. For insurance expenses, the balance will be $200 which represents one-month benefit utilized out of twelve months. We saw in this example how insurance expenses were recognized with the passage of time.

Let us see now another example for office supplies, its related cost will be recognized by the usage and consumption. On 2nd Feb 2019, the company paid $500 cash for office supplies which are expected to last several months. At the date of preparing financial statements which is 28th Feb 2019, the company counted the remaining quantities of office supplies and found a value of $400 is still on hand. In this case the use of office supplies is calculated by the difference between $500 and the value of remaining quantities $400, which result in $100 as supplies expenses.

To record this adjusting entry, we debit supplies expenses by $100 and credit office supplies by the same value $100. We can write an explanation "office supplies usage for Feb 2019". As a result of this entry, the balance of the office supplies account will be $400, which represents the remaining quantities on hand as of 28th Feb 2019. While the balance of supplies expenses is $100, which represents the usage value of these supplies. This is the end of our chapter, thanks for reading and see you with the next one.

Deferrals - Unearned Revenues

We learned in our previous chapter the first group of deferrals which is called prepaid expenses. We will discuss in this chapter the second category which is unearned revenues. When companies receive cash before services are performed, they record a liability which is called unearned revenue, such as airline tickets. The customer pays cash in advance, and sales value is recorded as unearned revenue until flight service is provided. Other examples are magazine subscription, rent, and advertisement.

During the accounting period, it is impractical to make daily entries as the company performs services. Instead the company delays the recognition of revenue until they prepare financial statements. This is the treatment for services. But what about materials? If we receive cash advance against sales of material, we will book it in the same way as liability which we call unearned revenues. This liability account will be offsetted to become sales revenues once these materials are delivered.

Let us now see the effect of adjusting entries on unearned revenues. Since liabilities are overstated and revenues are understated at the time of preparing financial statements, an adjusting entry for unearned revenues results in a decrease or debit to liability account and an increase or credit to the revenue account. After recording the adjusting entry, liability balance represents the value of remaining revenues to be recognized in future periods. To understand this subject let us have a look at a specific type of unearned revenue which is advertisement services.

Once the company receives cash in advance, it will be recorded as an increase of liabilities. So, what will happen at the date of preparing financial statements? We will record an adjusting entry by debiting unearned revenue and crediting advertisement revenue accounts. For example, on 1st Feb 2019 the company received $10,000 cash in advance against advertisement services to be performed in future. At the time of collection, the company will record this collection as liability which we call it unearned revenue as follows: we see in this example how cash account increased by $10,000 and unearned advertising revenue account increased by the same value of $10,000.

In the journal entry we debit a cash account and credit unearned advertising revenue account by the value of $10,000. We can write an explanation "cash advance for advertisement services' '. Now at the date of preparing financial statements on 28th Feb 2019, the company performs partial advertisement services for the value of $6,000 during the month of Feb 2019. We see in this case there are two accounts that get affected, advertisement revenue account will increase by $6,000 and unearned revenue account will decrease by the same value $6,000. In journal entry, we debit unearned advertising revenue and credit advertising revenue accounts by $6,000.

We can write an explanation "Advertisement revenue for Feb 2019". As a result of this adjusting entry, the balance of unearned advertising revenue account will be $4,000 which represent the remaining revenue value to be recognized in future periods once advertisement services are performed. For advertisement revenue accounts, the balance is $6,000 which represents the value of services rendered in Feb 2019. This is the end of our chapter, thanks for reading and see you with the next one.

Accruals - Accrued Expenses

After we learned deferrals, we will study in this chapter the first group of accruals which we call accrued expenses. So, what do we mean by accrued expenses? They are expenses incurred but not yet paid or recorded at the time of preparing financial statements. Such as bank interest and salaries to employees. So, companies make these adjustments of accrued expenses to record its obligations which exist at the balance sheet date but are not yet recognized. Prior to recording adjusting entry, both liabilities and expenses are understated. Therefore, an adjusting entry for accrued expenses results in an increase or debit to expense account, and an increase or credit to the liability account.

Let us have a look at specific types of accrued expenses. We will start with accrued interest. On 1st Mar 2019, the company signed a six-month note payable for the amount of $10,000. The note requires an annual interest rate of 6%. The maturity date of both the face value and interest must be paid after six months. So, how do we close our accounting period for the month of Mar 2019? We should record an adjusting entry for accrued interest as follows: we will start by calculating interest value for one month. This value is determined by three factors.

First one is the face value of the note payable. Second factor is the percentage of interest rate. Third factor is the length of time in terms of one year because we are using an annual interest rate. So to calculate the interest for the month of Mar 2019, we multiply the face value which is $10,000 by 6% which is the annual interest rate by the period which is one month over twelve. The result for one month will be $50, while total value of interest is $300 which is payable after six months.

Let us see now how to record the adjusting entry for Mar 2019. We notice there are two accounts that are affected. Interest expense will increase by $50, and accrued interest will increase by the same value $50. In the journal entry, we debit interest expense by $50 and credit accrued interest by $50. We can write an explanation "Accrued interest for Mar 2019". As a result of this entry, the balance of interest expense account will be $50, which represents one-month cost for Mar 2019. While the balance of accrued interest account is $50, which represent the liabilities for one-month to be paid at maturity date. So, what would be the journal entry at maturity date on 31st Aug 2019?

At that date, there is one-month unrecorded expense for Aug 2019, while five months expenses from Mar to July 2019 are already recognized in previous periods which are included in the accrued interest account. To record the payment entry at maturity date, we debit interest expense account by 50$, and debit accrued interest account by 250$. Why debit? Because to reduce a liability account, we record the transaction on the debit side. Then, we debit notes payable by $10,000. At the end, we credit the cash account by the amount of $10,300 which represents the total amount payable for both interest and the face value of note payable. We can write an explanation "Payment of interest and face value of note payable".

After this entry, the balance for interest expense account will be $300 which represents expenses for six months, while the balance of the accrued interest account will be zero after this payment. Let us take another example of accrued expenses which is accrued salaries. We will assume the company is paying salaries to employees on the 5th of each subsequent month. For example, the salary value is $2,000 for Mar 2019 which will be paid on 5th Apr 2019. In this case we can't close the Mar period without recognizing the cost of salaries. We record our adjusting entry by increasing both salaries expense and accrued salaries accounts.

In the journal entry, we debit salaries expense by $2,000 and credit accrued salaries by the same value $2,000. We can write an explanation "Accrued salaries for Mar 2019". As a result of this entry, the balance of salaries expense account will be $2,000 which represent the cost of salaries for Mar 2019, while the balance of accrued salaries account will be $2,000 which represent the liabilities to be paid on 5th Apr 2019. So, what would be the payment entry on 5th Apr 2019?

We debit accrued salaries by the amount of $2,000. But why debit? Because a reduction of the liability account will be done on the debit side. Then we credit the cash account with the same value of $2,000. We can write an explanation "Salaries payment for Mar 2019". After this entry, the balance of accrued salaries account will become zero after this payment. This is the end of this chapter, thanks for reading and see you with the next one.

Accruals - Accrued Revenues

We will study in this chapter the second category of accruals, which we call accrued revenues. So, what do we mean by accrued revenues? They are revenues earned by performing services but not yet recorded at the time of preparing financial statements. Accrued revenues may accumulate with the passage of time such as interest revenue, or it may result from services that have been performed but not yet billed. These services are not billed because only a portion of total services are performed, and the client will not be billed until all services are completed.

Prior to recording adjusting entry, both asset and revenue accounts are understated. Therefore, an adjusting entry for accrued revenues results in an increase or debit to asset account and an increase or credit to the revenue account. Let us take one example of advertisement services. On 31 Mar 2019, the company performed advertisement services worth $1,000 during the month of Mar 2019. The total advertisement services will be completed by 15 Apr 2019 with a total value of $1,500. So, how to close our accounting period for Mar 2019 without issuing the bill to our customer?

We should record an adjusting entry for accrued revenues as follows: we notice in this example there are two accounts that get affected. Accrued advertising revenue and advertising revenue accounts will increase by the same value of $1,000. In journal entry, we debit accrued advertising revenue by $1,000 and credit advertising revenue by the same value of $1,000. We can write an explanation "accrued revenue for Mar 2019". As a result of this entry, the balance of accrued revenue account will be $1,000 which represents the receivable value which is related to Mar 2019 and it will be billed in future.

While the balance for advertisement revenue account will be $1,000 which represents the partial value of services revenue for the month of Mar 2019. So, what will happen once all services are performed on 15 Apr 2019? The company is going to bill the client the full value of advertisement services for the amount of $1,500. In this case, a value of $1,000 was already recognized under accrued revenue account in Mar 2019. So, what is the billing entry to be recorded on 15 Apr 2019? We will debit accounts receivable with the full value of $1,500 and then credit two accounts.

The first account to be credited is accrued advertising revenue by $1,000 because this revenue was already recognized in Mar 2019. The second account is advertising revenue to be credited by the value of $500 which represents services value for Apr 2019. We can write an explanation "advertisement invoice for customer A". After recording this entry, the balance of the accrued revenue account will become zero. While the balance for advertisement revenue account will become $1,500 which represent the full value of advertisement services performed until 15 Apr 2019.

At the end, let us consider the client paid this bill on 25th Apr 2019. In this case, we debit a cash account by $1,500 and then credit accounts receivable by the same value of $1,500. After this entry, accounts receivable balance will become zero which represents the bill was paid in full value. This is the end of our chapter, thanks for reading and see you with the next one.

Adjusted Trial Balance

After posting all adjusting entries, companies prepare another trial balance which is called adjusted trial balance. It shows balances of all general ledger accounts after recording all adjustments at the end of the accounting period. The purposes of preparing adjusted trial balance are as follows. First, to prove the equality of total debit balances and total credit balances after adjustments.

Second, it is a primary tool to prepare financial statements since it includes all the data needed. To understand this subject let us see the following example of unadjusted trial balance for the period ended 30th June 2019. We can see in this example the trial balance starts with a cash account with a balance of $10,000. Then, accounts receivable with a balance of $2,000. A balance of $500 for prepaid rent, $8,000 for equipment, $1,000 for accounts payable, $15,000 for owner's capital, $6,000 for service revenue, $1,500 for salaries expense. The total debit and credit balances are $22,000.

At the end of the accounting period, the company recorded the following adjusting entries. The first entry to record accrued salaries for June 2019 by debiting salaries expense account and then crediting accrued salaries account for the value of $500. The second adjusting entry to recognize rent expense for June 2019 by debiting the rent expense account and then crediting the prepaid rent account for the value of $100. After we post these adjusting entries, we can prepare the adjusted trial balance. To make it easier to understand, we will add two more columns for adjustments and two more for the final balances after adjustments. Notice the affected amounts are highlighted in red color.

We can see there are two extra accounts added, the first one is accrued salaries and the second one is rent expense. As a result of the first entry, the salary expense account is debited by $500, and the accrued salary account is credited by the same value of $500. For the second adjusting entry, the rent expense account is debited by $100 and the prepaid rent account is credited by the same value of $100. Let us now calculate the balances after these adjustments. We will start with a prepaid rent account.

The balance of $500 is reduced by a credit transaction of $100 to become a $400 debit balance after adjustment. The second account affected is salary expense. The balance of $1,500 is increased by a debit transaction of $500 to become a $2,000 debit balance after adjustment. Third account is accrued salaries, which is increased by a credit transaction of $500 to become also $500 credit balance after adjustment. Our last account is rent expense, which is increased by a debit transaction of $100 to become also a $100 debit balance after adjustment.

At the end, let us see how adjusted trial balance will look like. You can notice the affected accounts are as follows: prepaid rent with balance of $400, a balance of $500 for accrued salaries, $2,000 for salaries expense, and $100 for rent expense. Notice the equality of total debit balances with total credit balances for the value of $22,500. The last point to observe is how we used the dollar sign in the first figure for each column and also in the totals. This is the end of our chapter, thanks for reading and see you with the next one.

Closing The Books

After financial statements have been completed, the company starts to make the accounts ready for the next period. This process is called "Closing" and it is done at the end of the current accounting period. Let us now identify the accounts for closing purposes, we have two groups of accounts: temporary accounts and permanent accounts. Temporary accounts accumulate data related to one accounting period only. They include all income statement accounts plus the owner's drawing account. So, why do we call them temporary? Because they are opened at the beginning of a period, and then used to record transactions related to that particular period, and then closed at the end of the same period.

These accounts are summarized as follows: revenues accounts, expenses accounts, and owner's drawing account. In contrast, permanent accounts are related to one or more future accounting periods. They include all balance sheet accounts including the owner's capital account. So, why do we call them permanent? Because these accounts are not closed from one period to another. Instead, their balances are carried forward into the next accounting period. These accounts are summarized as follows: assets accounts, liabilities accounts, and owner's capital account.

Let us now see the steps of the closing process. In general, companies use a control account to close revenues and expenses accounts. We call this account "Income Summary". But why to use a control account? This step is important to avoid recording excessive details in the capital account. In the closing process, temporary accounts are closed in permanent accounts, and the balances of all temporary accounts will become zero after closing. To illustrate this process, let us see the following: the first step to debit each revenue account for its balance and credit income summary with the total value of revenues.

Second step to debit income summary for the total value of expenses and credit each expense account for its balance. Third step to debit income summary and credit owner's capital for the amount of net income. If we have net loss, the entry will be the opposite by debiting the owner's capital and crediting the income summary. Fourth step to debit owner's capital and credit owner's drawing for its balance. After recording these entries, the balances of all temporary accounts will become zero, and these accounts will then become ready to accumulate data in the next accounting period which is totally separated from the previous period.

The closing process we saw right now is applicable for proprietorship and partnership companies. But what about corporations? In corporations, we use different equity structures and the closing process will change accordingly. In this case, temporary accounts will not be closed in the corporate capital account. Instead, they are closed in different equity accounts which are called "Retained Earning". Why do we call it retained earnings? Because its balance represents the value of net income left over after distributing dividends to stockholders.

To illustrate this process, let us see the following: we notice here income summary and dividend accounts are closed in retained earning rather than corporate capital account. This process is specific for corporations which is different from proprietorship and partnership. We will focus in this Book on proprietorship companies. This is the end of our chapter. In the next chapter we will practice the closing entries with examples. Thanks for reading.

Closing Entries

After we learn the closing process, we will study how to record closing entries in our books. To understand this subject, let us see the following example of adjusted trial balance for the period ended 30th June 2019. At the beginning, we will identify the accounts for closing purposes as temporary or permanent accounts. Remember that temporary accounts are revenues, expenses, and the owner's drawing account.

While permanent accounts are assets, liabilities, and the owner's capital account. In this example we have the following temporary accounts. Service revenue, salaries expense, insurance expense, supplies expense, and owner's drawing accounts. Next, let us see the permanent accounts. We have a cash account, accounts receivable, prepaid insurance, equipment, accounts payable, accrued salaries, and owner's capital accounts. To start the closing process. We will follow these steps. First, we close revenues to income summary.

Second, we close expenses to the income summary. Third step, we close the income summary to the owner's capital. Fourth step, we close the owner's drawing to the owner's capital account. Let us start with closing revenue accounts. We debit service revenue accounts by $5,000. But why debit? because revenues normally have credit balances and to make these balances zero we have to record debit transactions to close them. After that, we credit the income summary account by the same value of $5,000. The second step to close expenses accounts is as follows. We debit income summary accounts for the total value of all expenses which is $3,000. Then we credit salaries expense for the value of $2,000 and insurance expense for the value of $500, and then supplies expense for the value of $500. But why do we credit all these expenses? Because expense accounts normally have debit balances, and to make these balances zero we have to record credit transactions to close them.

Let us move now to our third step. We notice the income summary account has one credit transaction of $5,000 and one debit transaction of $3,000. As a result, net income value is $2,000. To close this balance, we debit the income summary account by $2,000 and then credit the owner's capital account by the same value of $2,000. After this transaction, the income summary balance will become zero. Remember that if we have net loss, the closing entry will be reversed. Owner's capital account will be debited, and the income summary account will be credited. Let us now move to our last step to close the owner's drawing account.

We debit the owner's capital account by the value of $1,500 and then credit the owner's drawing account by the same value of $1,500. But why credit? Because drawing accounts normally have debit balances and to make these balances zero we have to record credit transactions to close them. After recording all closing entries, temporary accounts balances will become zero and the capital balance will represent the total equity balance of the owner as follows. We notice in our example there are two closing entries affecting capital balance.

One credit transaction of $2,000 which come from closing income summary account,

and another debit transaction of $1,500 which comes from closing the owner's drawing account. As a result, the ending balance will become $15,500. This balance will be shown in both the balance sheet, and the statement of changes in equity. The last point to observe is the income summary account. This account is used only in the closing process. We are not using an income summary account to post any transaction during the year. This is the end of our chapter. In the next chapter, we will prepare the trial balance after closing. Thanks for reading.

Post-Closing Trial Balance

After posting all closing entries we can prepare another trial balance called post-closing trial balance. This type of trial balance lists permanent accounts and their balances only, since all temporary accounts balances become zero after closing. The purpose of post-closing trial balance is to prove the equality of permanent accounts balances, which are carried forward into the next accounting period. It provides evidence that the company journalized and posted closing entries properly.

It also shows the accounting equation is in balance at the end of the accounting period. Remember that, this balance of total debits and credits does not mean the records are free of errors. Still there are some types of mistakes that may exist. For example, a transaction is not journalized and posted at all. Another example, a transaction is posted twice. Let us have a look at our trial balance before closing. This example is taken from our previous chapter.

Notice that the following temporary accounts will be closed, and they will not be shown in post-closing trial balance. These accounts are owner's drawing, service revenue, salaries expense, insurance expense, and supplies expense accounts. Let us now prepare the post-closing trial balance, which will contain permanent accounts only. We will start with a cash account for the balance of $10,000.

- Accounts receivable with a balance of $3,000.
- $1,000 for prepaid insurance.

- $6,000 for equipment.
- $3,500 for accounts payable.
- $1,000 for accrued salaries,
- and finally $15,500 for the owner's capital.
- Total debit and credit balances are $20,000.

This equality means all permanent accounts are ready to be carried forward for the next accounting period. Remember that this is only applicable for proprietorship and partnership companies. For corporations, there is a different equity structure and the closing process will change accordingly. This is the end of the chapter, thanks for reading and see you with the next one.

Reversing Entries

After preparing financial statements and closing the books, some accountants prefer to reverse certain adjusting entries at the beginning of the next accounting period. Each reversing entry is the exact opposite of the adjusting entry made in the previous period. The use of reversing entries is an optional process in the accounting cycle. The purpose of using reversing entries to simplify recording a subsequent transaction related to an adjusting entry. For example, a payment for interest expense related to current and previous periods resulted in debiting two accounts.

Interest expense for the current period and accrued interest for the previous period. With reversing entries, we can debit the whole payment to the interest expense account. To understand this subject, let us see the following two examples. We will start with an accrual account which is accrued salaries. In our example, a company is paying monthly salaries every two weeks. This payment is done based on five days per week. On 27th Sep 2019, the company paid $10,000 for salaries incurred between 16th Sep and 27th Sep 2019. The payment entry is recorded by debiting salaries expenses and crediting cash accounts for the value of $10,000.

The second entry will be recorded on 30th Sep 2019. At this date, there is one day accrued salaries for the value of $1,000 which will be paid on 11th Oct 2019. The adjusting entry is recorded by debiting salaries expense and crediting accrued salaries for the value of $1,000. Our third entry is done also at the end of Sep 2019 to close expenses accounts by debiting income summary and crediting salaries expense account for the value of $11,000. Our last entry on 11th Oct 2019, the company paid $10,000 for salaries incurred between 30th Sep and 11th Oct 2019. Out of this value there is $1,000 related to accrued salaries.

As a result, the payment entry will debit two accounts salaries expense by $9,000 and accrued salaries by $1,000. Then the cash account will be credited with $10,000. Let us see now what will happen when we use reversing entries. Notice the first three entries in Sep 2019 are the same whether we used reversing entries or not. On 1st Oct 2019, we will use a reversing entry which will be the exact opposite of the original adjusting entry. In this case, we will debit accrued salaries and credit salaries expense accounts for the value of $1,000. So, what will happen at the time of payment? We will record the whole cash payment as expenses by debiting salaries expenses and crediting cash accounts for the value of $10,000. This is where reversing entries becomes handy by debiting an account as expenses rather than debiting multiple accounts. After recording payment entry, the balance of salaries expense account will become $9,000 which represent the value of salaries incurred between 1st Oct and 11th Oct 2019.

On the other hand, the balance of accrued salaries account will become zero because we have one credit transaction on 30th Sep and another debit transaction on 1st Oct for the value of $1,000. Let us now move to another example for a deferral account, which is office supplies. On 1st Oct 2019, the company purchased office supplies for the value of $8,000 by cash. In this case we debit office supplies and credit cash account for the value of $8,000. On 31st Oct 2019, the company found there is still $3,000 value of office supplies on hand. In this case, we record the adjusting entry by debiting supplies expense and crediting office supplies for the value of $5,000.

At the end of Oct 2019, we will close expenses accounts by debiting income summary and crediting supplies expense accounts for the value of $5,000. Let us see now what will happen when we use reversing entries. Remember that while using reversing entries we record the whole cash payment as expenses. In our example on 1st Oct 2019, we debit supplies expense and credit cash account for the value of $8,000. On 31 Oct 2019 when the company found there is still $3,000 value of office supplies on hand we debit office supplies and credit supplies expense accounts for the value of $3,000.

After recording this adjusting entry, the balance of supplies expense account will become $5,000 which represents the cost of supplies used during the period. The balance of the office supplies account will become $3,000 which represents the quantities of supplies which are still on hand. At the end of Oct 2019, we will close expenses accounts by debiting income summary and crediting supplies expense accounts for the value of $5,000. So, what will happen in the next accounting period?

We will record a reversing entry on 1st Nov 2019, which will be the exact opposite of our adjusting entry. In this case we debit supplies expense and credit office supplies accounts for the value of $3,000. After recording this entry, the office supplies account will become zero, and the company will continue to record the purchases of office supplies as expenses while another adjusting entry will be recorded at the end of each subsequent period. At the end, remember that this process is totally optional in the accounting cycle. Since both ways will have the same ending result, the company may choose the more suitable process to follow. This is the end of our chapter, thanks for reading and see you with the next one.

Conclusion

The balance sheet is a snapshot of a company's financial position at a specific date. Up to this point, we learned unclassified balance sheets whose items are grouped into whose items are grouped into assets, liabilities, and owner's equity. To improve users' understanding of a company's financial position, it is preferred to use a classified balance sheet which groups similar assets and similar liabilities using standard classifications.

One of the more important classification is the separation between current and non-current items for both assets and liabilities as follows. Under assets, we group them into current assets and noncurrent assets. Each group lists a specific type of account. For example, non-current assets list long-term investments, property plant and equipment, and intangible assets. Under liabilities and equity, we have three main groups. Current liabilities, non-current liabilities, and owner's equity.

We will see in this chapter the accounts that are listed under each of these groups. But before that, we need to learn something called the "operating cycle". This is important to understand the rule behind separation between current and noncurrent assets or liabilities. So, what do we mean by operating cycle? It is the time span from the payment of cash to acquire goods and services until cash is received from sales of these goods and services. For a service company, it starts with paying salaries to employees who are performing these services until cash is collected from customers.

For a merchandise company, it starts from paying suppliers to acquire inventory until cash is received from customers. In general, the operating cycle period is less than one year. This means most companies use a one-year period in deciding which assets and liabilities are current and noncurrent. In this regard, a classified balance sheet lists current assets before non-current assets, and current liabilities before non-current liabilities. Items in current assets are listed in the order of how quickly they will be converted into cash, while items in current liabilities are listed in the order of how quickly they will be paid by cash.

Let us start with the first group, which is current assets. They are assets that a company expects to convert into cash or to be used within one year or its operating cycle, whichever is longer. Such as accounts receivable are current assets because they are expected to be collected within one year. Another example is inventory, which is classified as current assets because the company expects to use them in operation or to sell them within one year. Let us now have a look at common types of current assets. Such as cash, short-term investments, accounts receivable, inventory, and prepaid insurance.

In the balance sheet, these assets are listed in the order in which they are expected to be converted into cash. Cash account is listed first because it is the most liquid item, while prepaid expense is listed last because it will not be converted into cash. Instead, it will be expensed during the period. Let us move to the second classification, which is long-term investments. They are usually the following. First group is investment in stocks and bonds, which are expected to be held for more than the longer of one year or operating cycle. If these securities are expected to be sold within one year, they will be classified as short-term investments.

We have also in our list long-term notes receivable and long-term assets such as lands and buildings which are not used in operating activities. If they are used in operating the business, they will be classified under our next classification which is property, plant and equipment. They are tangible assets that are both long-lived and used in operating the business, which are expected to generate future economic benefits. Such as lands, buildings, equipment, and furniture. These assets are reported in the balance sheet at cost minus accumulated depreciation. So, what do mean by depreciation? It is the practice of allocating the cost of the asset among its useful life.

Note that depreciation is an expense account which will be reported in the income statement. So, what about accumulated depreciation? It is an account that shows the total amount of depreciation that a company has expensed so far in the asset life. Notice that lands are not depreciated because they are assumed to have unlimited useful life. Let us now move to our next classification, which is intangible assets. They are long lived assets that don't have physical substance. One famous example is goodwill. Other examples are patents, copyrights, and trademarks which give the company exclusive right of use for a specific period of time. These intangible assets are amortized among the period of exclusive right of use.

Our next classification is current liabilities. They are obligations due to be paid or settled within one year or the operating cycle, whichever is longer. Common examples are accounts payable, notes payable, income tax payable, accrued salaries, accrued interest, unearned revenues, and short-term bank loans. It also includes any portion of long-term debts. Current liabilities are reported in the order of those items to be settled first. Let us now move to our next classification, which is non-current liabilities. They are obligations to be paid or settled after one year or operating cycle, whichever is longer. Such as bonds payable, long-term notes payable, long-term bank loans, and pension liabilities.

If a company has both short and long-term items in each of these categories, they will be separated into two accounts in the ledger. Our last classification is owner's equity. The content of this chapter will vary depending on the legal form of the business. For proprietorship, there is one capital account. In partnership, there is a capital account for each partner. For corporations, the equity chapter is usually divided into two accounts: common stock and retained earnings. For a retained earning account, it is affected by two items, net income or loss and dividends. This is the end of our chapter, thanks for reading and see you next time.

Don't miss out!

Visit the website below and you can sign up to receive emails whenever ADIL KHAN publishes a new book. There's no charge and no obligation.

https://books2read.com/r/B-A-GZFBB-WENRC

BOOKS 2 READ

Connecting independent readers to independent writers.

Also by ADIL KHAN

Business Strategy Understand What It Takes To Be Successful In Business
Emotional Intelligence Gaining Control Over Emotions
Project Management - Complete Guide For A+ Project Managers
Accounting 101 Learn The Basic Principles The Right Way

www.ingramcontent.com/pod-product-compliance
Lightning Source LLC
LaVergne TN
LVHW022203200926
848481LV00006B/1825
* 9 7 9 8 2 2 3 5 7 5 5 8 0 *